Cowboys & (

Poetry from the T

Brick Street Poetry Inc. invited poets from Indiana and around the world to contribute poems inspired by authentic cowboy cocktails for this anthology: *Cowboys & Cocktails: Poetry from the True Grit Saloon.* This anthology was published in conjunction with an NEA Big Read partnership with the Eiteljorg Museum of American Indian and Western Art in Indianapolis.

See the recipes for the authentic cowboy cocktails mentioned in many of these poems at the end of this book.

Barry Harris, Editor

Cowboys & Cocktails is published by Brick Street Poetry Inc., a tax-exempt non-profit organization under IRS Code 501(c)(3). Brick Street Poetry Inc. publishes the Tipton Poetry Journal, hosts the monthly poetry series *Poetry on Brick Street* and sponsors other poetry-related events.

Cowboys & Cocktails: Poetry from the True Grit Saloon

Acknowledgments

In 2019, Brick Street Poetry joined with the Eiteljorg Museum of American Indian and West Art and the Indianapolis Public Library to present programs as part of an NEA Big Read Grant. We were most pleased to have three poetry events included in the three months of "True Grit" happenings. For the first of the poetry activities, we choose to assemble this anthology which we titled "Cowboys & Cocktails, Poetry from the True Grit Saloon" and which we debuted at Saloon Night at the Eiteljorg on April 25th. For May we invited former Indiana Poet Laureate Shari Wagner to lead one of our *Poetry Alive* Workshops for children at the Eiteljorg and invited rancher and North Dakota Poet Laureate Larry Woiwode to read at the Eiteljorg in June.

We have partnered with the Eiteljorg on quality programs in the past and were pleased to join them in this Big Read programming. In addition to the NEA's support, Brick Street would like to acknowledge the support of two other exceptionally generous funders who helped support the "True Grit" poetry activities through grants supporting Brick Street Poetry's activities. We are thankful for program support from Indiana Humanities and the National Endowment for the Humanities and for operational support from the Allen Whitehill Clowes Charitable Foundation during our planning stage.

Contents

Cowboys & Cocktails: Poetry from the True Grit Saloon

Lone Tree Cocktail

Joseph Heithaus

2 liqueur glasses dry gin
1 liqueur glass french vermouth
2 dashes maraschino

Fill a mixing glass with ice, add the above ingredients, stir well, and strain
into a cocktail glass. Twist a small piece of lemon peel on top and add the
peel to the cocktail.

Imagine under the glassy sky
a lone tree,
a cottonwood shedding
its limbs onto the painted desert floor,
a noose hung from a branch
or an arrow stuck in the trunk,
the sun howling above.

Fill your picture with horses, women, and men,
add some movement, a boy dashing across the dust,
someone hurling a tomahawk or shooting a gun.
Stir well.
And strain into a thousand grainy films depicting pieces of this scene—
a lot of cowboy hats, and shiny boots, plenty of horses and feathers
and painted skin spinning under a sound track of rumbling hooves
and primal cries.
It's all in black and white
and the whites, for the most part, always win,
though a few go down for effect, and the black
is mostly in the eyes of the people left behind,
call it fear or fire or fire water.

Twist in some bitterness toward manifest destiny and pray we're all destined
for some other fate, some manifest
of ingredients that might make people one,
and add that lone tree
with everything else peeled away,
no noose or arrow,
no trace of any human touch.
Then drink it fast and find in the bottom of that empty glass
some other past
or future where the earth
is whole again.

1

Golden Slipper

Joseph Heithaus

Gold is why you slipped
across the prairie's snow,
wind cutting through your duster with each blow.
You watched the heaps of bison grip
the icy silence of the earth
until those steely mountains gave birth
to biting hardships you never dreamed you'd know.

But you crossed and found a little vein
and mined it just enough to have some nuggets in a safe
so now you sit at the Elixir on 16th
still feeling at times the chafe
of the saddle and those three fingers you lost to frostbite.   Their pain
hangs in San Francisco's foggy air beside the wine glass
you pinch with thumb and pointer, the two digits left behind.

The *Golden Slipper* has no ice. The Chartreuse, you're told,
is gauzy yellow and Goldwasser is German for *water made of gold.*
You love to watch him add what you like to call the sun,
an egg yolk your tender bartender never will let run.

This is the heat you've tendered from the ground
some dainty shoe of warmth against the cold. You're rich now.
Buy another round.

Whiskey Daisy No. 3

Joseph Heithaus

after *Off for Town*
   by Charles Schreyvogel (American, 1861-1912)
   Eiteljorg Western Collection

Off for Town, they arrive to tie their horses
to the saloon's hitching post, then spur
the wooden sidewalk and swing
through swinging doors to sidle up
past brass spittoons to sit at the burly bar.

They aren't ordering a Whiskey Daisy No. 3—
one wine glass whiskey
and then imports from across some lazy tropic sea—
lemon juice and pineapple syrup, even powdered sugar
are, for cowboys, foreign as peacocks and elephants.

In the painting one boy from his sorrel points—
left hand on the reins, his Smith and Wesson Model #3 Revolver
with his right—right at you.
Even the horse's eye widens white and frights
at how that bullet's headed toward your chest.

That cowpoke drinks his whiskey straight from the bottle he just bought.
Halfway through, he feels again his pointer pulling back,
and sees spinning through the blue a round of lead,
some stray crow spooking at the pistol's crack,
then from your heart a blood-red daisy blooms you dead.

The Voting Women's Punch

Doris Lynch

I always remind my husband we're partners, not landowner and serf,
boss and bossee. After rattling, half-dragging our stagecoach

across the continent, we drive cattle on and off the range. Here
in the Colorado Rockies, we of the female persuasion, demanded

schools for our young but the bachelors said, "No. Over our dead
bodies." When we pushed back, they ponied up for only three months,

can't afford no fancy-dress teachers, no primers, no blackboards. At quilting
and sewing bees, we decided we needed to vote for the school board.

Hell, run it! So we marched and hollered. Outmeetinged their meetings.
Still we know it was only our suspension of baking sweets that toppled

their resistance: we plumb ran out of berry cobblers
and applesauce cakes. Not a single molasses or sugar cookie

could be found in the county. Relenting, the gold miners allowed us
to vote though, in fact, we were owed it. In November of 1893

we became full citizens for the first time. Amazingly, we kept the vote,
not like neighboring Utah, where the men passed it in '70, reneged seven

years later before it finally stuck to the books in '96. Having elected a few
fine women to the legislature, we new voters decided to ring in the Fourth

with a festive beverage. Ivy Jane Thompson, saloon owner and celebrated
Kansas City cook, recommended *Rocky Mountain Punch*. No matter

that among us we had only one ingredient—a quarter bottle
of rum that Jeanette had liberated from under her husband's side

of the cornpoke mattress. For maraschinos we tossed in gooseberries,
the same ones that stained our husband's flannel shirts when we

went picking. The color, a lovely burgundy-port, the men would assume
they spilled while imbibing after we exhausted women trundled to bed.

Canvassing every sod and wood-framed house in the county, we found
only a single uneaten Christmas orange, its skin, puckered—nowhere

near purty--but capable of lending the needed hint of citrus. All across
these hills and valleys, not a swill of Champagne could be found,

4

so we raided our husbands' stashes of spiked cider. Meanwhile, Ellen
located a mineral spring, so we splashed a few gallons in the barrel

for added fizzle. The fellas drank and drank that punch. When we
told them we nicknamed it *Rocky Mountain Deceiver*, they looked first

at each other and then slowly at us wondering God knows what.
But we womenfolk knew why and wherefore we came

to celebrate. Let them wonder about their *Deceiver*
while we'll hang tight to the *Rocky Mountain Punch*.

Rocky Mountain Punch
5 bottles Champagne
1 quart Jamaica rum
1 pint maraschino
6 slice lemons

Sugar to taste. This delicious punch is compounded as follows. Mix the above
ingredients in a large punch bowl and then place in the center of the bowl a
large square block of ice. Ornament it with rock candy, loaf sugar, sliced
lemons or oranges and fruits in season. This is a splendid punch for New
Year's Day.

A Widow's Missive

Doris Lynch

~ *Clark's Fork Bottom, Montana, 1881*

Pardon, Jake Roberts, although a ranch wife
for twenty-one years, for me a pony is still
a frolicking, miniature horse with ears soft
as a Boston lady's leather gloves, yet your recipe
calls for not one but three partial or full ponies.
The bitters, I understand--angostura or other.
Life has shared far too many sorrows with me.
The twins died of diphtheria on the wagon train out,
leaving only our boy, Leroy who lost a leg helping
with plowing. Then last January 10th when Tim
returned from the saloon, corduroy jacket
bleeding red, and fell before me, heart stopped
on our threshold, snow turning crimson beneath him,
I had to drag him inside. Later his left hand formed
a claw, that I feared not even the devil could release.

I could have used your fancy drink then during
the undressing, bathing and the covering with his blanket,
the one Tim had saved from his beloved stallion,
Lucky Clover. Its scents of horse and tobacco
no wind or rain could release. Could have used
a stiff one during that 10 p.m. ride to O'Shawnessey's
ranch in the dark, coyotes lapping at my skirts
in that field of downy brome and spring wheat.
Any moment, I expected one of the beasts to gnaw
my boots—scuffed and years worn. Now you send
this wrinkled note on your wife's dry goods list—
hopefully fulfilled—"Darlin, wil ryde bi Freiday
with fixns for a Widos kis." Yes, please, bring your ponies
—both full and half, your flask of amber brandy,
the Benedictine gargle juice—praise be the good fathers!—
but stay, Mr. Jake, on the other side of the screen
door for this widow is all kissed out.

The Sad Tale of Dancing Gals at the Tarantula Bar and Snakebite Cafe

Doris Lynch

Sicker than piss-fed dogs or plum-drunk
cattle, none of the girls looks dressed for dancing
when I arrive at the Tarantula Bar and Snakebite Cafe.
Resting, sure enough, the only thing happening today.
I suspect too much of last night's bug juice or coffin
varnish, but Adelaide, the only gal who can gargle
a few words, mentions fever, muscle aches, headaches
the size of the Chiricahua Mountains and tummies
more spun than tumbleweed in a February windstorm.

Still wearing my riding pants, I drag over the scarred
cooking pot, pour in the ale, add a few sprigs of nutmeg,
then measure molasses--brown sugar's scarce
in these parts—and set it a-boiling. Between bedroom
moans and girls rushing past, pantaloons hitched high,
to the outhouse, I whip egg whites, fork-flick the yellows,
then slowly, steadily, the way Pop Stinney taught me,
fold them into the bubbling mixture, careful not
to let it coagulate or turn puke yellow.

"Yard of flannel," I yell to the girls but they want
none of it. Instead, at the sound of "yard," their bellies
wrench, so I cheat calling it a tipple of flannel. "Flame those
flu bugs away zapping your innards. Get your breakfast too
with these here egg flips. A mere draught well set your stomach
straight 'cause no way can I dance alone tonight, no way
these long legs can kick up a fancy Parisian can-can without
you dimpled cowgals beside me, sharing smiles and winks,
leaning toward the pit where the men slip wooden nickels
between our breasts, and gaze at us with eyes the size
of the wagon wheels that carried us all west."

The Night Paul McCartney Jilted Me at the True Grit Saloon

Lylanne Musselman

Sultry and single, I was
looking for a little sexy mischief
when I crossed the crowded saloon,
and I saw him standing there.

Those gorgeous hazel eyes,
a wild crop of hair, he spoke
of his revolver, laid it on the bar.
"I'm Paul," he said with a grin,
"I'm a lover, not a fighter."
I swoon, swoon, swoon.

He ordered an Old Chum's
Reviver. "We'll dance after this one,
love," he chortled. I slid closer,
drinking my second Yellow Dog
cocktail, trying to act sober.

We stumbled to the dance floor,
and held each other tight,
he was everything I hoped for,
even though he was too polite.
Suddenly, he leaned in and whispered,
"Do you want to know a secret?"

My heart fluttered as I felt
him falling for me. Instead,
he said, "I'm crazy for making music."
His humming in my ear I'd misread.

He waltzed me over to the corner,
I sulked, while he sat making up
silly love songs about riding
off into the sunset and such.

"Love, love, love is all you need…"
Yeah, yeah, yeah. He winked at me;
I slammed back my fifth Yellow Dog,
drunk and mad - I'm not being tickled and
played like that brash, upright piano.

A Saloon Girl's Lament

Lylanne Musselman

The west tears a woman's heart apart as she learns to live,
with grit, lye, and lies. Women are expected to be pure.
The priggish people oppose my life in the saloon,
when I let down my hair to laugh, dance, and drink

with grit, lye, and lies. Women are expected to be pure,
instead I enjoy my hard-earned Maiden's Blush,
when I let down my hair to laugh, dance, and drink.
My spirits are lifted with a strong absinthe and gin.

I toast the rough men with my hard-earned Maiden's Blush,
after a few, all cowboys look tall, strong, handsome.
My spirits lift higher with a strong absinthe and gin,
the saloon becomes my dance floor in a mighty spin,

more and more cowboys look tall, strong, and handsome.
Fancy women look down their noses and call me "shady lady"
because the saloon becomes my dance floor in a mighty spin,
never mind many sweet, good men are not here for love.

In the streets, fancy women take to calling me "shady lady."
So many priggish people oppose my life in the saloon,
never mind the sweet, good men are just passing through;
the gritty west tears a women's heart apart as she learns to live.

9

To Kiss a Cowboy

Mary Sexson

I could never kiss
a cowboy
without the fine blend
of desires caressing
my tongue, loosening
my lips, my nostrils parted
just enough
to sniff his breath, smell
the timber of his pitch,
the lean of his longings.

No yellow dog will breach
this maiden's blush,
nor break through
the stone fence
around my heart,
built strong enough
to stop
a Jersey cow.

This maiden's kiss
is a life-prolonger,
it is passion's solar plexus,
the golden fizz of sunrise
hitting us
like a Rocky Mountain punch.
My cowboy's yard of flannel
is draped around us both
as we sip together
from this golden slipper of love.

The sensitive cowboy

Joan Colby

Not my last rodeo, he says
Excusing himself for the act of caring
When a shrug suits his mood
Or more specifically his pose.
Somebody wrote a book condemning
The traits of masculinity: ambition,
Aggression, the swagger
Of boots down the boardwalk.
In the True Grit Saloon, he wants
A shot and a beer, but instead he orders
Today's special: the Maiden's Blush.
He's a sensitive cowboy if that's
What it takes now. You've gotta
Be careful with the spurs or the
Spanish bit or with the words
That give you away like a drink
You're meant to savor. Men
Used to keep things together
Stuffed in saddle bags. They stuck a foot
In a stirrup and rode away
To someplace safer.

Ranch Morning after the Glorious Fourth

Maureen Tolman Flannery

Hey Mom, do you think the rodeo boys got back?
They tied it on so wild at True Grit Saloon
that they're not yet even stirring in the shack.

Them Bar-H boys were fixing to bushwhack
our guys some no-moon night when storm clouds loom
and I'm not sure if the rodeo boys got back.

The bunk house door is open by a crack
and squeaks on rusty hinges, but the room
is quiet. Aint no snoring from the shack.

They've all been teaching me to stay aback
the wildest broncs that I'm learning to groom.
I wish the rodeo boys would just get back.

The cook's whipped up a mess of his best flap-jacks.
He'll throw 'em to the dogs before high noon.
I don't like the funny quiet in the shack.

I think it's best I set out now to track
the road they take around the river dune.
It's awful quiet in the bunk house shack
and I don't think the rodeo boys came back.

Trespass

Maureen Tolman Flannery

We, I keep reminding myself, are all trespassers,
we white Christian takers, making our way in the west

explorers who discovered what had never been covered,
the first British cattle barons who learned to churn
      free grass through cattle into cash,
all the rough-edged drovers trailing longhorns north
      up from Texas expecting a chance at a ranch of their own
each Mormon elder who knew to redirect water
      through dry soil to coax up food
every toiling sheepman's wife, feeding her brood
      from a sheep wagon stove and working herds beside her men
each homesteader who planted family and future
      onto a hillside with a creek or spring
especially we who grew up here, entitled through ancestral names
      that enable us to call *home* the land our grandparents tamed.

All of us usurpers. This land belonged to itself
and herds of wild animals that traversed it.
The only rights the land might recognize—Cheyenne,
Arapaho, Shoshone—made no claims of ownership
but knew themselves to be stewards.

Their current home, now shared with former enemies,
is an inhospitable slice of vast lands the roamed.
Yet they're dared to subsist there
on obliterated histories and the grand gamble.

13

Full as a Tick at the Buckhorn Saloon

Carolyn Kreiter-Foronda

Been ridin' all day to get here to forget
the long hours herdin' and ropin' cattle,
the desert dry as a fever. Nothin's been wet
for months, so at sunrise I straddled

my horse, and like a high-falutin' dude
took off for the Buckhorn Saloon
to wet my whistle and elevate my mood
with whiskey, a couple tablespoons

of sweet cider, and two or three lumps
of ice. I order a second glass to boost
the spirits, a third glass, beef clumps,
a bowl of beans, and then whoop

it up with some leaky-mouth stranger.
The effects of more glasses of *Stone Fence*
pump up my heart 'til I'm in danger,
so I start airin' the lungs in defense

of this hog killin' time. Full as a tick,
I gamble. To avoid rotgut, I request
the *Glorious Fourth* – no need to be sick.
Gum syrup, ice cream, lime juice: a rum-fest.

Pumped up, I could tame a field of wild
horses, be a first-class Bronco Buster.
All I need's homemade whiskey. I smile
as I toss Lincoln skins to the bartender,

the cluster of paper money snatched up
like gold, gamblers brawlin' in full swing
as I exit, cup my feet into the stirrups
and like a wailin' loon, start yodeling.

His (Whiskey) Daisy

Justice M. Cundiff

His green eyes danced as he leaned forward on the counter.
"Pour me the usual, sweet thing," he drawled.
"It reminds me of you."
It was my job to oblige, so I did just that.
I even made my best effort
To ignore his crude comments when I turned my back.

I poured pineapple syrup,
The same shade of gold as the braid down my back.
Lemon juice splashed into the glass,
Just as bitter and sour as my disposition.
I mixed it with powdered sugar
That was nearly as sweet as my dimpled smile.
And I mixed it all with a shot of whiskey
That was as dry as the gunpowder for my revolver.
I kept it tucked into my garter for men just like him.

His lopsided grin fell on me when I returned with his glass.
"Would you look at that," he chuckled,
"I've picked myself a daisy."
But we were both well aware
That I was more whiskey than daisy.

Yard of Flannel

Eli Cleary

There are miles of moonlight between here
and the loom. Here, where sheep spread out
over the hillside like constellations
beneath the ghostly silhouettes of cowboy
and canine - their gaze fixed on the fields.

Before the shearing, comes the threat
of the culling. There is a rhythm to it.
Not like the gentle rake when carding the fleece,
or the steady beat and whirl of the spinning wheel.

Nightfall brings a dance.
The warp and weft of coyote and dog,
weaving an intricate pattern
in and out of the flock.
The coyote howls. The ewes bleat.
The dogs come bye
and away - demand fidelity.

Keeping the sheep true requires obedience
as they comb rough edges smooth,
find and cast strays into the fold -
else the frothing coyotes
would have their wool
bloodied, forever staining
the softly flannelled pattern
they weave.

Corpse Reviver
Terry Kirts

"Suddenly, the reader will be surprised to hear, every man jack of the company of troopers gets excessively drunk and incapable on a couple of enormous stone jugs of some American drink."

      - *Lloyd's Weekly Newspaper*, October 23, 1859

Back before cough syrup, before Ovaltine,
before Americanos served by baristas
with Garibaldi beards, you could lean
against mahogany or brass and knock
two ponies back for breakfast, harsh
as the night you didn't die from.
Come in from the cattle trail and taste
some mustache tickler reimported
from Paris, what the British thought
we drank: brandy matched with cherry,
made medicine by cardamom and clove.
We'd stand right there while the train
still rumbled on. Then catch the caboose.
Two if we'd lost a woman or a bet,
but four would un-revive you in a jiffy.
The books don't have us right.
That stuff about two pistols drawn
at noon? We wanted our free lunch:
oysters and celery, radishes and cheese,
all the dainties that would lure us in,
linens on the tables we'd count cards on
once the sun hung at the prairie's end.
We'd pull our guns to make a man dance,
but who doesn't like a floor show now
and then. Every generation wants
its fixer. Even you need a barstool, too.

Drink Diretory

Stephen R. Roberts

To assist you in ordering from the extensive, lecherous libations of the True Grit Saloon

Corpse Reviver

A few of these and you're out tapping tombstones,
sifting through zombie shadows, whimpering to savor
flakes of any unusual late-night, low-fat TV snacks.

Maiden's Blush

Brings back buggy rides and froggy-went-a-courtin'
recollections of a renegade ancestor who fell out
of your family tree and off the wagon the same night.

Yellow Dog

More than one of these and the pound goes wild.
Mongrels, cast-off puppies, and three-legged curs gather
to finish a canine quick-step across a hound-warped floor.

Lone Tree Cocktail

A grand choice for those few and far between
who want to stay that way, with their sudden urges
and tendencies to frolic in the upper branches.

Yard of Flannel

With six eggs and ale, it's best to arrive in checkered
pajamas or a cross-hatched lumberjack shirt, ready
to mingle upside down with a length of plaid chickens.

Jersey Cow

There's nothing quite like getting Old Bessie sloshed.
Every Wednesday is Bring In the Family Cow Night.
One per household. Two shot minimum. With cash-prizes.

**For more on these and other choice beverages,
holler for your waitress.**

The Rainmaker

Chuck Wagner

The drum that once
Spoke of thunder
Hangs silent on the wall
Like the head
Of some stunned animal,
And the rockets
That startled clear skies
Like lightning
Like dormant
In the damp cellar
Dreaming of the smell
Of sulfur.

On the back stoop
Of a long-neglected house,
The rainmaker rests
His ramshackle body against
A bent wood rocking chair,
Sleeping off a night of Stone
Fences in the heat
Of a Kansas drought,
A crooked stream
Under a cloud
Of white hair.
Intermittently, a forgetful
Hand searches a scraggly
Beard for a trace
Of tar and feathers.

Doc Holliday and Big Nose Kate Share One Last Balaklava Nectar

Rosemary Freedman

This is how I remember it. I was the nurse called to care for Dr. Holliday. The same man who, on horseback, would slowly turn his head to give me the once-over. Here he was drowning in the same consumptive creek that his mother died in when he was 15. TB, the "white plague," him 36 looking every day a hundred. Pale as water's shimmer. His reformed, often backsliding, prostitute, common-law wife, Big Nose Kate, sitting there on the edge of the bed, with their even-to-even IQs. Anyone with sense knew that's what drew those two together. Men always chasing whores — but I'm a nurse, so I'm not going to judge.

His body and the room permeated with a smell you could taste for two weeks. A smell that would follow you like a ghost. The smell of rotten meat and abscess mixed with vinegar, metal, cheap perfume and cantaloupe. Kate sharing his favorite drink -- balaklava nectar -- him, sipping through coughing spells, leaning in to kiss her goodbye, calling out the numbers of the teeth in her Hungarian laugh, like on the study charts from the dental school. Kate always coming and going out of his life through Kansas, South Dakota, New Mexico. He spills the drink and Kate kneels on the squeaky floor to wipe the pine boards clean. She tells him she will be back soon, that she's going to get one last balaklava nectar. Then she motions for me to step into the hallway, her brown wet tangled curls sticking to her face. She mouths "I can't be here" and she has a tortured look as she holds in the noise of her weeping, her nose running. It was just then I understood how oddly and exquisitely beautiful she is. She staggers down the stairs towards the resonating pink Colorado sun.

The stories of him eviscerating card cheaters ride incongruent with the picture of a 20-year-old boy graduating from dental school before he is old enough to practice. The man who planned to die with his boots on, friend to Wyatt Earp and his brothers, resident at Fly's Photography Studio and boarding house, sharpshooting, gun slinging, fast drinking, boozing boarding-house owner. Gambler, boy without a mother, still mad at his father for remarrying too soon, ribs as bare almost as a desert carcass, the balaklava nectar staining the dressing gown and new white sheets I just put on the bed in the small room with pink flowers on the wall. A broken kaleidoscope with all the colors missing, he can't even reach for a cloth to spit in, much less a gun. Rings sliding off his fingers, me wanting to keep them. This is the part of the hero I will never divulge to anyone. The frailty, that cough that resonates through the November wind like an ancient echo of the dying.

I shave him finding the shiny scar from a repaired cleft lip. His dull milky blue eyes staring in the shadowy shimmering of light falling through windows. I cut his nails, flatten down his cowlick, then I pray over him, whether he would want it or not. I think of how he used to look at me when I was younger. Now he is sinking like a man in quick-silver. Doc, your last drink is with me. Far from the sweet cocktails you are used to and a multitude more intoxicating. This sweet bitter nectar that allows your breath to quiet. Oh, laudanum, laudanum, though you be bitter you are to be highly praised. I give him his wish: I put his boots on, one last time before his final inhalation extinguishes all the little fires in his lungs.

Ghost Town: Rhyolite, Nevada

Alexis Ivy

One grave, the girl who died here.
She wasn't buried

with the wedded Christian women
but by the saloon/ brothel/ jailcell
side of town because she was

the one who slept with husbands.
This is a town once lived in and left.
No one leaves with their belongings.

So much people walk away from.
The reason for the place all used up
miners boomtown in 1906, prospect for gold
and taken away from the place.

All that's here of a bathhouse
just the claws of the tub, scabs in the dust.
and the placard on the front door:

extra ten cents for clean water.
The hills thirsting, drink before I can.
The unlivable survives.

Every tree a Joshua tree
waving help or good day.

Without Rain

Alexis Ivy

When it, if it, it will happen
I can't pick a day. The ground
keeps all for itself. Leaves
no trace. Land lives through,

reckons with it. I watch a storm
makes its way to my camp.
Took the stars out of my sky.

So far away. Time enough
for three more logs on the fire.

In the desert I can tell you
what the sky will do,
the distance. It is always
about the rain until the rain.

The Yellow Dog
Vienna Bottomley

Is a straight chaser.
He treads softly behind
Wagons, his tail tucked
Low like a timber wolf.
His callused paws scatter
Copper-headed quail
That shudder across the
Buffalo grasses beyond
The old road. At dusk
His eyes glow orange,
and, by night, his bark
Fills the barren spaces,
Cracking the heavy
Silence like a cowhide
Switch.

Despite the Doldrums
Joe Bisicchia

In a desolate corner of Nevada, here,
ever still,
she has an unquenchable presence.

I return here daily and dodge tumbleweed
to watch her rise from her long deep sleep,
and I breathe in all the coolness of Sierra.

Not just words on an old poet's page,
or ripples on a faraway desert stage,
not just unseen history gone in the wind,
not just some rodeo as a shooting star,
but presence, here, the very breath within,
as she swirls all the cosmos.

Others may reminisce, but I call her Hope.

For every cowboy dreams of the new day.

24

A Dark Valentine for Hannie Caulder
Michael Brockley

I'm drinking my third Widow's Kiss in the shadows of the True Grit Saloon. You paid for the funeral of the man who taught you to lose when you win. The bounty hunter who said a man should leave something behind besides a tombstone. The sunset casts a long shadow in the desert towns along the border. Until the difference between a desperado and a preacher of fallen angels is the size of the buttons on a wrangler's duster and a revelator's waist coat. In the street, watch the gunslinger's eyes. Kill the fastest man first. Move as soon as you pull the trigger. I'm still nursing the third kiss, a drink mixed too bitter for my taste. I dig the graves you buy with your dead-or-alive bounty. And play a harmonica on the edge of town so the shooting stars know when to spread their rumors. You will ride a dapple grey across the horizon with Lucifer's redeemer in your wake. I will leave you someone else's song. Any man can steal a Bible.

For the buck
Merlin Flower

disappointed, she made a
'glorious fourth' cocktail
 adding brandy, jamaican rum,
ice cream and lime. and smile.
Followed by a thrilled shake to the
core. another smile.
Easing of the first word
 in this poem.
she danced.

Cowboys

Rosanne Ehrlich

Was she two? Three?
She could have been older but
her parents claimed she sighed his name in her sleep.
Was it "Geeene" (a sigh here?),
"Geeeene" (perhaps another sigh there).
That was a long time ago, people would say,
but for her it was like yesterday.

Then, in the living room, listening to the radio,
the words of the song telling her,
in that honey-rich voice,
the other reindeer used to laugh and call him names.
They wouldn't let poor Rudolph play
in any reindeer games.
It brought her to tears.
Was she 5? Maybe 6?
She knew one thing for sure.
She loved Gene Autry.

He was "The singing cowboy".
She was sure that many women
who grew up listening to the radio
found him attractive. He and Roy Rogers.
But Roy was married to Ginger.

It was the era of the cowboy.
Once a year, the rodeo came to town
Cowboys gently led prancing horses
through the sawdust, around a ring,
they swirled circles of rope above their heads
and over the necks of bucking steers
and serenaded cowgirls, Annie Oakley,
or one of the many other cowgirls
who all seemed to be named Annie.

Then every weekend
all the neighborhood kids would escape
into the rough-and-tumble life in the "Old West"
of the Saturday matinee movies.
A quarter covered admission and a five-cent pack of candy
from the vending machine in the lobby.
Under the direction of the "matron" with her flashlight
they would find their seats to watch
packs of men on horseback riding through the desert,
passing the same big rock formations every week,
kicking up the same sand.
Then shootouts in the middle of a town's dust-filled street
always alternated with scenes in the True Grit Saloon
where frequent fist fights would break out after
too many Golden Slippers or Maiden's Kisses
over old wounds or imagined slights
or cheating at card games.
It was our Star Wars.

Years later, when walking through a department store
during the Christmas holiday,
Gene Autry sang to her,
singing about Rudolph
with that sliding, honey voice.
And one day,
she met a real cowboy,
a guy from a small town in Colorado.
He called her Darlin'.
Close enough for that cowboy fan.
Thanks, Gene Autry

A Maiden's Blush Can Kill a Man

Ron Wallace

"What the hell did you just ask for?"
the bartender's voice graveled the air.

One boot on the brass rail,
leaning up against the old oak bar
a dusty cowboy sipped his beer
and eyed the stranger
from beneath the Stetson's tilt.

"A Maiden's Blush,"
The dude repeated in a haughty manner.
"It's all the rage in New Orleans."

The cowboy took another swig
        of his luke-warm beer and grinned.

"Old Tom gin, a little absinthe, a lemon
        Strawberry syrup
some powdered sugar, over cracked ice.
My God, what kind of salon is this?"

Wiping out a mug, the bartender growled,
"We're closer to El Paso, Texas,
than to New Orleans
        just in case you didn't notice;
whiskey or beer, take yer pick."

"I'd ford the Phelegethon on a stone blind pony,
I'd kiss a rattler on the lips
        before I'd drink
the swill that man is drinking."
He gestured at the cowboy.

The cowboy smiled
        sat down his mug of beer
                drew his .44
and shot the dude between the eyes.

"Don't know if you've got a pony,
but you best get to crossin' that burnin' river
      while I cross the Rio Grand,"
the cowboy laughed
and poured out the dregs on the bleeding corpse.

"But, Sam,
you better pour me one more before I go."
He grinned at the barkeep.
"Damn it, John Wesley
      that's the third one this month.
You gotta find yerself another way
to argue with a man."

He placed another beer in front of the cowboy.

"Maybe so, Sam, maybe so
      but I can't tolerate
some fancy Dan talkin' down my brew."

He downed the beer in one long draught.
"See ya in a week or two
      viva, Mexico."

Tale of a Wild West Saloon Girl

Shirley J. Brewer

I left New York burlesque, headed West.
Never even looked back, knowing
normal was not my way of life. I wanted
a taste of the wild surging inside me.
For days I traveled by steamboat and rail,
arrived at last at the True Grit Saloon.

Here's what you need to swallow:
I could sing, dance, flirt. And I could
mix a drink strong as the varnish
on a dead man's coffin. No feller
played with my ruffled petticoats without
permission. I worked as a saloon girl,

poured cowboy cocktails and tongue oil
whenever the bar dogs took a break. I tucked
a jeweled dagger between my breasts
to keep the boisterous boys in line.
Fell in love with a saddle slicker
from Sioux City. Smokin' Joe gave me

a pink gemstone garter that made us blush.
Two fuddled gunslingers shot him up
for no good reason. A brave piece of calico,
I rose to the rescue, concocted the most
potent drink in the house. *The Corpse Reviver.*
1 pony each brandy and maraschino,

2 dashes Boker's bitters. Orange peel
stings a man back to life. Truth tell,
not a chance of serving that juice in a glass.
I doused Smokin' Joe's face until his lips
turned pinker than my garter. He snapped
out of it, bought me a diamond ring to match.

Three Bartenders of the Old West

Shirley J. Brewer

At night three ghosts rise from a swirl of dust
in the bone orchard at the edge of town,
gently topple a marble tombstone to make
a temporary bar. Those lost boys—all
died young—have mastered the ethereal
art of conjuring. Bottles appear in prairie air,
multiply below the slick coaster moon.
The spirits gather ingredients, prepare to

compete. Pistol Pete pours *The Life Prolonger*,
everyone chuckles at the irony. He shakes
sherry wine, port wine, sugar, cream, egg.
Strains his potion into tall glasses. Serves.
The thirsty bar dogs swallow. A bit tipsy,
they howl their sorrows at the powdered moon.
Flannel John goes next. He grabs gin,
French vermouth, maraschino—takes his time

twisting lemon peel for his *Lone Tree
Cocktail.* The wind warbles like a drunken
cowboy. Gunslinger Gus wipes away a tear,
mixes a *Widow's Kiss,* his memories fresh
of a woman who buried two husbands yet loved
only him. His hands tremble over apple brandy,
yellow chartreuse, ½ pony Benedictine. Before
he adds the bitters, the boys bow their heads.

Three dead bartenders. No one wins. The wind
turns intoxicated, mean. The moon a saloon girl,
a drug to soothe their wounds and garnish loss.

On Understanding a Language That is Not Your Own

Christine Donat

Y-intercept and Middle Finger walk into a bar—
the former says "I came here searching for my X,"
the latter laughing at the line reiterates to piss-off.
Elbows greased in tap-beer and soggy tip money,
F-Sharp waits for a date who decides not to show
                              a tempo too slow.
A-roll and B-roll try to make sense of the act
between Frida and her Flat-Brush—the films
arguing her intermission that came too quick
              "we'll take two Maiden's Kiss."
Hieroglyphic draws a similar conclusion
with a shot of house tequila—no salt and
no lime. Beaker leans over the counter
fast—to steal booze while the bartender
stays focused on the beauty of Flask.
A free buzz off barkeep's distraction,
he doesn't know they work together
                      how clever.
Alexander Pushkin's lost poetry
sulks in the corner, then orders
Balaklava Nectar at last call
              a round for all.
Then Time rolls his dice
making four AM strike:
all will leave the bar
drunk in anguish,
framed only by
their own
language.

The Fort

Melanie Browne

My dad and Uncle built
it from the ground up
and it had a trap door
for keeping out
the Indians or
the Cowboys or
other siblings,

you could spend
the night in it
if the weather was
nice and look up
into the night sky,

We fought each other,
& shot them DEAD,
which is a term
that might not
pass muster
any longer

but you had to die
slowly
and painfully
which helped kids
understand not
death exactly
but the art
of pretentiousness,

if we had been thinking,
we might have given them
a pretend
sip of Corpse Reviver
so they could have
gotten up much faster

Eventually as time
wore on it came down,
the wood splintering
and ending up in our fireplace,
the backyard now
With ordinary patio furniture
But still littered with
imaginary bodies

Stone Fence

Connie Kingman

Once, side by side and full of joy,
they built the cabin, tended fields and herds, grew a family,
their life sweet mortar binding them.

Now, only silence between them,
not a word ever spoken of the indiscretion.
Though they choose to honor their commitment,
anger and remorse rob them of their joy.

Today at the pasture, stacking small boulders
upon the last course of a stone wall,
perhaps it is the call of a bird across the prairie,
perhaps the breeze tousling her hair as she kneels to steady a stone—
he sees anew, like a dream revealing, and turns toward the cabin.

There, pouring what little bourbon is left
from the bottle she had given him two years ago
on his fiftieth birthday, he tops it off with sweet cider,
pressed from apples of the trees planted on their wedding day.

Returning to the field with a goblet awkwardly cupped in his palm,
she watches. His stride stirs a memory; she recalls a young man.

With his free hand, he reaches for hers;
pulls her up, away from the stone fence;
takes a sip then offers the glass to her.
Though unsure, she accepts, meets his eyes, and sips.

34

Tethered to the West
Elizabeth Krajeck

An American life is to ride West,
first as a child on a rocking horse,
then a 1930s cowgirl,
leaves the woodlands, rides over grassland

across America on her
Harley Scrambler, wearing
a helmet, leather jacket, and trousers,
carrying a tent, knife, and journal

she seeks the Miami remembering
Indiana, the Omaha in Nebraska,
reaching drought and switchgrass in Kansas,
she rides with dust and wind

among the Cherokee in Oklahoma,
the Navajo in Arizona,
snow and cowboys near Utah,
stopping at the True Grit Saloon

where after repealing Prohibition,
Colorado ranchers listen to the cowgirl's
story about how she was
raised in rooms behind a bar

near the Red River,
not far from church and school
on Highway 10 in the Dakotas,
and while she talked,

tethered to the West, she listened
for the click of bar glass with a drink
called the "Stone Fence" and while she tasted
bourbon whiskey and sweet cider

on magnificent ice,
she told how she planned to be a writer,
sad that her first pencil was a spoon,
until inspired she wrote on True Grit's wall:

Another word for paper is land; another
word for land is pure, glacial water.

Looking Back at House Made of Dawn

John Irvin Cardwell

I do not run in the desert
Nor bare of feet, not on rocks,
Thorns, or sun ablaze streets.
No, I do not do these things
Nor descend into a kiva for wisdom.
My diet is short on true local corn,
Perhaps, it is void of such.

I run in my dreams, and in them
I explore the deserts, ascend the mountains,
Descend the streams, and run,
And run again until I am back in the Midwest,
Negotiating forest shaded trails,
Smelling the woods in fall,
The decay of leaves and nut husks
The rising of living elements in mud and dust,
The stirring of those in creeks and puddles.

I am old now.
Perhaps, I can talk to N. Scott soon,
Share items in a pipe, share common
And uncommon dreams, feel the warm
Of the lifting sun as it warms us.
We will look back at our houses
In the dawn, share the hope of pollen
And hope for all animals including humans
As our words and laughter are hope for us.

The Only Things

Claude Clayton Smith

Go places,
see what's there;
fool around and
grow my hair:
These are the only things
I care about.

Pocket money,
just enough;
duffle bag
with all my stuff:
These are the only things
I care about.

Stone Fences,
Widow's Kiss;
spend the night
in blurry bliss:
These are the only things
I care about.

Music playin',
children, too;
maybe someday:
me and you.
These are the only things
I care about.

Grandpa Benno on the Karl May Express

Norbert Krapf

One winter in southern Indiana, my Grandpa Benno
shut down his steam-engine sawmill and threshing machine,
as usual, but this time headed out from little St. Henry

for the Wild West and some time on Easy Street, Texas,
where the large saloons, he heard, were open and Cowboy
Cocktails were lined up to be served. How did he get there

from southern Indiana? My father, who was born in a room
above a saloon across the street from the village church,
told me his father headed down the road to the nearby

Johnsville Station, caught the Karl May Express,
and rocked the rails all the way West down to Texas
all by his lonesome. Dad said he sent postcards back home

telling folks he loved the winter weather there and those
lip-smackin' Cowboy Cocktails he could not stop sipping,
instead of the good beer he quaffed in that saloon run

by his father-in-law, August Luebbehusen. You could say
those cocktails were a special winter treat for Grandpa Benno.
He claimed in a postcard he had one, not a Manhattan,

that made his mustache tingle! He gave its name
as A Maiden's Kiss. How could it not tingle if you
see the ingredients he wrote down in a handwriting

that looked like old German script: first a Maraschino,
then Crème de Roses, White Curacao, Yellow Chartreuse,
and some of that Benedictine the monks served over

at St. Meinrad Archabbey not all that far down
the road from St. Henry. Yessir, you try a Maiden's
Kiss and tell me it doesn't make your white mustache

turn black again! Try and tell me a cocktail like that
won't make you rock down the rails on the Karl May
Express as you sit in the white-oak rocking chair

you made by yourself and relax, to devour the fiction
of Karl May in German and tales about the friendship
between Old Surehand, the white cowboy, and Winnetou,

Chief of the Apaches. Don't complain to me that the young
Karl May, born of poor weavers, went to prison for stealing
six candles and later stole a watch and lost his teaching license,

then turned to writing well-researched best-selling novels
depicting a rare brotherhood between races and championed
world peace. Even though he never made it to the American West,

he did reach Buffalo, New York. Look, I believe in the power
of the imagination and the pen as having the potential to serve
as a tool for brotherhood and harmony. Just a minute, dear

reader, here comes that A Maiden's Kiss I ordered. My
gray mustache has started to tingle. Sit yourself down!
I ordered it for you. You ready for the Karl May Express?

Sam's Widows

Cheryl Soden Moreland

The spurs on his Tony Lamas scrape the wooden barstool
As he teeters backwards balancing on one leg
Laying his handsome head against the lead-painted wall
Tipping his woolly tan Stetson over his dark, deadly eyes

Other cowboys enter the swinging saloon doors
Ready for their end-of-day rewards
Hired hands with their callouses and blisters
Deserving of a tall cold one or several

Sam orders his usual Widow's Kiss
Chugging it down his dusty throat like the last quencher
Around those parts surrounded by mountains
Smothered in kisses from a blazing sun

He rises from the wobbly table
Walks upon the creaky, splintered planks
Towards the scorching outdoors
Where his quarter horse waits

A man women want and men want to be
He's also a man with an aching body
But with mouth moistened and belly full
Ready to jump on Ol' Jackson

Who will take him across the prairie
To plant another blazing kiss
On the lips of a lonely widow
Waiting with patient yearning

For her long lean mustachioed Wyoming wanderer
As she shoos flies from her holey screen door
The one he promises to fix every time he comes
Promising to visit

Wild Spirits

Marlene Million

~ after "Maiden's Blush" drink

Riding upon her wild, white Mustang,
Cowgirl canters towards True Grit Saloon.
Her horse used to roam free
amid winds whistling through
Tonto National Forest.

As the horse ran and bucked
recklessly in training corral,
she worked feverishly, determined
and succeeded taming her Mustang.

She earned respect with folks
and local cowboys. She was ready
for a fanciful drink's concoction
of botanicals nurtured in her herb garden.

The intense absinthe, aromatic
with sweet fennel, anise, and wormwood,
was grown fresh. Bartender mingled magic
with glorious gin and red raspberry syrup.

Added ice, juicy lemon, powdered sugar
were shaken into a frothy mixture.
A rose-colored glass awaited
Cowgirl's toasting with drink divine. . .

"Raise 'em high for Spirit, yippee-ki-yay!"

John Muir's Salvation
Shari Wagner

~ "John Muir, noted naturalist and conservationist, founder of the Sierra Club and 'The Father of our National Parks,' spent a brief, but life-changing time in Indianapolis."
—Dawn Mitchell, *Indianapolis Star*, February 18, 2014

I rented a room
at the crossroads of America,
confident I could stand
with one foot on a factory floor
and the other, among the trees.

But I couldn't stretch that far.
Within a year, I was sucked
inside *the rush and roar and whirl*
of Osgood, Smith & Company,
consumed by the ingenuity
of my inventions, automations
that assembled the hubs, spokes
and rims of wheels.

But the labor I saved others
cost me time in the forest,
my precious excursions
constrained to Sunday afternoons.
Efficiency polluted my ambitions,
narrowed me into a channel,
like Pogue's Run
that slipped past the shop, doomed
to be subverted, pulled
under tall buildings. I was engulfed
by the machines I created
and they wouldn't let go—

till March 6, 1867, at the corner
of Illinois and Merrill. Tightening
a mechanical belt, my metal file
slipped and flew like a loosed arrow,
piercing the cornea of my right eye.
In sympathy, the other drew dark:
a total eclipse.

For weeks I collided
against furniture, confined
to a darkened room, blind as Jonah
swallowed by the whale.
In that deep cavern, I heard
the universe breathing, without
and within, calling me
to join Nature's workplace,
eternal wellspring of Beauty.
I resolved to live among
the trees I had abandoned
whether or not I regained my sight.

By grace I was spit out into sunlight
with newborn vision.

I left Indiana on foot, following
overgrown pathways and riverbanks,
sweet fields of tickseed and larkspur,
waves of giant bluestem and what leafed out
from crags and crevices, rumors of glaciers
etched in rock. I was a mountain man
hitched to his walking stick,
drunk on the Golden Fizz of sunrise
and the Maiden's Blush of sunset
reflected on Yosemite's snow-capped peaks.
Sequoia stood as columns of sunshine.
I slept under a roof of stars
and worked each day with a view
from a thousand windows.
Heart to heart. Dust to dust. Cheek to cheek.
Dissolved and absorbed. Never alone
unless my pride dammed the flow of spirit.

And so I come down from the mountain today
and say, Go outside, children of Nineveh,
into the wilderness of your true home. Escape
the gears and screens that distract you. Turn
toward the living universe—pulsing
rivulets, radiant and leaping,
all creation diffused yet together
in the cataract's
rush and roar and swirl.

The Conversation

Michael Keshigian

Jack Daniels called to me,
in my stupor, from behind the bar,
shouting out from a long line
of liquid male monikers,
beckoning my attention
from the shelf
upon which he rested,
said he could mix up some sweet cider
and eliminate the sensation
of feeling like I rode a stone fence all day.
So he lassoed my glass
and I validated the taste,
adding a couple of lumped cubes,
spending the night thereafter with Jack
as we attempted to pickle
my broken heart, shredded to pieces
beneath my slumping ribs.
I explained how I gave her my dream,
he laughed then burped,
how I gave her my breath,
he smirked and burned my throat,
how she raised my spirits
toward the highest of clouds,
he gagged and made me heave
my pathetic disposition
toward the busy barkeep,
obviously amused by
the one-sided conversation
until I redressed him.

Friendly Fire

David Alpaugh

By the time I was ten years old
I had shot every boy in our neighborhood

multiple times—and a few girls as well—
with my Roy Rogers cap gun.

> There was a real bang.
> Whiff of gunpowder.

Our *bad guy* for the day (Jerry, say)
would clutch his chest and groan....
Then, as if to prove cap guns *lethal,*
slide slowly down the trunk of oak
or maple, muttering, "Ya got me!"

They weren't bad guys. They were my friends.
I hadn't killed them. But I knew I could have
had my gun been a Colt or Smith & Wesson.

I too was shot many times. Twice, right
through the heart by a Dale-Evans-like
cowgirl who slid her silver pistol back
into her pretty pink holster and watched
triumphantly as *Jesse James* bit the dust.

Ya got me, Dale. Tell Roy I'm done for.

Today's suburban streets are eerily empty.
No tag. No hit the bat. No duels in the sun.
Though once in a while there's a drive-by.

Cap guns are passé. Imaginary shootouts
at ok corrals (on real streets) no match for
video games that boast hundreds of kills
per minute. *No one pretends to get hurt.*
Unlike Jerry & Doris & Tom & Eustace
(and me) digital images cannot pretend
to feel pain or be killed by friendly fire.

Once in a while, a lad who never got to play
with a cap gun brings *the real thing* to havens
named for playgrounds... beaches... flowers...

Parkland   *Sandy Hook*   *Columbine*

45

Hard Day
April Waldron

At four in the morning I get out of bed
Make a thermos of coffee to go,
The cows need milking, the chickens need fed
Rows of potatoes to hoe.

I walk to the barn through dew covered grass
My dog walking right at my feet,
I start up the tractor and fill it with gas
It's time for the horses to eat.

The stalls are now empty, I've gathered the eggs
Now to get tools from the shed,
Dog hair and cobwebs all over my legs
A feather was stuck to my head.

It's finally time for the sun to come up
I sit to enjoy a short break,
Pour me some coffee and sip on a cup
As the fog Rises up from the lake.

The day felt much longer because of the Heat
Sweat feels like fire in my eyes,
Needing a shower and something to eat
Then go have a beer with the guys.

I get in my truck and head into town
Can't wait to taste something cold,
The radio up and the windows rolled down
The sunset looks like solid gold.

I met with my friends at a bar called "The Brink"
The man at the bar seemed quite old,
With a smile he asked what I wanted to drink
I said I'd take anything cold.

He saw I was tired from working all day
And he walked to the end of the bar,
He proceeded to serve me the old-fashioned way
From a frosty cold quart Mason jar.

46

Slowly he poured and gave me a grin
And said "if you drink all of this",
"You won't remember how bad your day's been"
I call this a cold "Widow's Kiss"

Just a few drinks was all that it took
My body began to get limber,
He wrote my address in a black leather book
And that's the last thing I remember.

Lily goes West, young, to the True Grit Saloon
Bonnie Maurer

Behind the bar she fills a tumbler with chopped ice.
Adds absinthe and gin. She stirs
in a teaspoon of raspberry syrup.

Durango cowboys in to the cowboy bar.
His hands are big
and soft as Lily's breasts.
He wears his eyes
        like green bullets
                deep
                set
                upon Kitty
I mean Lily.

Lily licks the powdered sugar on her spoon.
She downs the Maiden's Blush.
Lily tumbleweeds over.
                He unbuckles his guns.

Saloon Goer

Joseph S. Pete

The sun-baked and plains-battered cowboy sidled up to the bar
after another rough, exhausting spat with the cattle.
"I'll have a Corpse Reviver," he loudly proclaimed,
casting a sidelong look round the room
to see if his reach at sophistication had impressed anyone.

He was a man of few means and fewer niceties,
but he had long been roaming the open range
and heard a few things about a few things
amid the rustling, wide-open grasslands.

"You'll have a whiskey,"
the saloon keeper countered,
pouring the leathery oak-brown liquid
into a smudged opalescent glass,
somewhat automatically.

"I'll have a whiskey,"
he announced just as boldly, knocking it back,
puckering a bit, wincing at the burn,
but letting the warm comfort wash over him.

He knew it wouldn't be long before
he'd be back out roughing it on that grass-patched rangeland,
choking down whatever the chuck wagon had that moonlit night,
gazing out over the endless shrubs and forage,
longing for the bitter, tingling kiss of liquor in the next saloon.

Golden Fizz

Kenneth Pobo

A neat cowboy, I don't let dust
build up. Give me unfancy clothes.
Any horse is my friend. A horse
is a house that dreams live in.

When I enter the saloon,
I'm usually tired. I like talking
with others like me unless they're
bags of belief. I have beliefs
I tend like the rose bush
in front of the hotel. Big red blossoms
explode and fade. I don't hold on
to truth too much. It withers. So,

I order a Golden Fizz,
prefer Old Tom Gin to whiskey.
Egg yolk thickens it like a drawl.
A couple of these and I'm ready
to put on the night and drop
into bed. Alone,

it gets tiresome, but the drink's
aftertaste calms and comforts.

Prairie Song or A Cowgirl's Lament

Robin Michel

You have lassoed my heart.

I lie down upon the warm prairie sand,
coarse like an old, wool saddle blanket
against my skin, and wish it were your cheek
I rest upon—the stubble of your unshaven face,
prickly like cactus against my thirsting flesh.

The yellow dog sun bleeds its passion
against ochre hills, washing the desert sky
in its untamed longings

And the cry of the coyotes are as plaintive
as midnight notes plucked from the steel strings
of a lonesome cowboy's guitar when there is only
the moan of the wind, the wail of his song, and
the glitter of stars to remind him of home.

As pressing as the strong and binding ropes
you've wrapped around my heart
failing to restrain its wildly beating desire
which roams this endless prairie night
riding fast upon my feral dreams.

Her lessons in social drinking
Laurel Smith

They still warn daughters
about crystal cups before
the dance: hell to pay in
nine months for all the good girls
tricked by Rocky Mountain Punch.

"Golden Slipper" sounds
like a game for grown-up
play: with a buzz, you're
Cinderella and he's a prince
until the frog of dawn.

Which is why I like
tequila straight with salt and
lime, no sweet mixer:
I see you, you see me and
we know what we're riding into.

The Creed of the Unnamed Men
J. Nguyen

Sentimentality:
Pay them ghosts no mind.
Keep movin' on forward and tippin' no winks

Man and Beast:
Truth be told, only you and your beast
Can truly talk about countin' the stars and makin' deals with good folk
The way that you want to - no contestin' and no ear bendin'

Rest:
No such comforts as true
As sittin' down with a bottle o' bourbon
Fixin' yourself a Stone Fence with big-as-flint-rocks ice chunks

51

Maiden's Blush
Thomas Alan Orr

I didn't know Sam Cass too well – nobody did.
We knew he brought in more outlaws than any marshal
in the history of the territory – several stretched over a horse
for daring to draw down on him. Lord, he was fast!
Carried a forty-four caliber Smith and Wesson Russian –
same as Pat Garrett – a mean piece of iron!

He retired here in Brimstone. The wife Tilda,
she was an invalid, you know, and he tended out on her
day and night. I always remember she liked that fancy drink –
what was it – Maiden's Blush – gin and sweet and sour stuff.
She was a beauty, despite her illness. They were a pair
all right, her and Sam, tall and dark. He was part Comanche.

Summers he'd carry her out to the porch – put her in a rocker
where she could see the colors on the mountains change
with the sun. Sam had an appaloosa mare – pretty thing,
soft mouth, nice gait. Tilda loved that horse and he'd bring her
up to the porch where Tilda could feed her sugar cubes.
They had some good years out here in this hard country.

It was cool that day Sam lit the stove, leaving Tilda
in her rocker bundled in a blanket while he rode into town.
Coming back, he saw the smoke and galloped hard
toward the house all in flames. He rushed to the porch,
reaching for Tilda, but the skin of her hand slid off like a glove
as she fell into the fire. A thing like that changes a man.

Afterward he was seldom seen in town, a solitary figure,
distant, lonesome, like a single tree in an empty field.
Folks would say hello but stood back from his grief.
When he did come, he always put his Bible on the bar
and ordered Maiden's Blush for Tilda. He'd down it quickly
and then nurse a beer for an hour or two.

52

One day a stranger walked in, dusty and thirsty
from the trail. He was young, hard-eyed, twitchy,
with a pearl-handled revolver slung low on his hip.
He ordered whiskey and stared at Sam on the corner stool.
"I know you, old man," he drawled. You're that marshal
what killed Joey Ballard!" But Sam just ignored him.

The kid stood up and walked over to Sam, saying:
"Hey, I'm talkin' to you!" And Sam: "Lower your voice, son."
"Like Hell!" the kid persisted. "Joey was my brother!"
Sam's eyes bore straight through the kid as he said:
"Joey Ballard was a stone cold killer. He had a choice.
He could have surrendered or come back ridin' stiff."

The kid pushed Sam's Bible on the floor.
It fell open and the skin from Tilda's hand,
pressed flat as a dry flower, fell out.
I'll tell you it got real quiet in there. Sam stood
and knocked the kid down with a single blow.
He picked up the treasure and put it back, real gentle.

Two big cowboys dragged the kid out to the street.
Sam finished his beer and walked outside.
He tucked his Bible in a saddle bag on the appaloosa
and heard the kid yell from the middle of the street.
"We ain't done here, marshal! I aim to settle
this account right now, so come out here and face me!"

Sam stepped from the shadow of the building.
He squinted at the sun. A crowd gathered. He said:
"You don't want to die this way, son. You got any kin?"
The kid laughed. "I killed six men already, old man!
You're next!" He made his move but Sam's Russian came up
so fast the kid never touched his gun.

The shot shattered the kid's hand and he went down
screaming. Sam said: "Reckon you won't be usin' that hand
to shoot anyone else." You could say it was a kind of justice –
a hand for a hand – the way that kid disrespected Tilda.
We watched Sam mount the appaloosa and ride out.
We went inside and had a round of Maiden's Blush.

A View from the Bank

Kyla McDaniel

You won't meet me
again under the apple tree at Weber's Creek.
Instead you make excuses
and sit in the saloon on a Wednesday night.
Drinking bourbon whiskey and cider, a Stone Fence,
Gambling for bits.

You'd never gamble on being seen
with a native
like me in this mining town,
bustling with hopeful
eyes from the east.

Perception from others worries you,
the potential gossip from folks
while watering their horses
or strolling to the mercantile.

You won't gamble on feelings you knowingly insinuated
while we walked
along silted banks that spring.

I'd carry my cedar basket full
of yellow lichen,
collecting for the healer in my tribe.
My reasoning to frequent the shady water.
Until the day I saw you looking
for gold.
I gave you beads as a greeting.

This became the norm weekly,
The "looking"
until the town was bursting.

You buried your emotions
in the muck of that creek.
Leaving me to hope
I'd strike it rich.

Cowboys & Cocktails: Poetry from the True Grit Saloon

Panning day after day
back breaking work
sifting and filtering
reasons and assumptions.

Your trepidation leaves our encounters empty
like the screen in your tin pan.

Cheeks wet
like the hem of my dress
floating in the water
not a fleck of remorse from you to be discovered.

Now you keep your distance
building a stone fence
on your lips,
like your drink of choice

On the next new moon
I will walk into that dusty saloon,
after panning in a different creek,
finding my gold in nuggets, heavy
as the water rushed over my toes,
cleansing my soul of your coercion.

I too will order a Stone Fence
this golden elixir.
Drink it down while you watch,
pretending not to know me,
your indigenous one.

I'll take the bottom of my dress
to wipe my mouth
as I leave a nugget on the bar.

Then you will know
the feeling of a wall being built,
a man-made barrier
of rough stones fit tightly together,
after a great expansion
has occurred in one's chest

Idaho Legend: The Hour Before

Trent True

The Hour Before

her village was attacked, the dawn
tried to warn her with crying sunflowers.

After she made an invocation,

the brittle wind carried her voice
across the mountains.

Those who are due to pay,
don't realize they are private prey

My death sentence stalks them
like a slithering prophecy.

The street is desolate, rejected by its companion,
 a petite tumbleweed.

The night's solace is tainted in this town
Somehow, the whores know, this one..
This night, is different. They're not around
to ply the hired guns.

One of them sloppily kisses his shot glass
filled with brandy, Corpse Reviver mix–

He thinks he recognizes me from a poker game
only he won't be getting any more chips –
I play my hand
A Remington, with its four of a kind

His friend has gone to Boise
to collect the rest of the gang's pay –
The hotel lounge with it gilded damask
wallpaper- a smart place to decamp, for a killer

The bartender is the only soul to take note of me
"Hello friend, you look like you're a Maiden's Blush man."
I give him a few dollars and he disappears.
Someday, someone will write a ballad about a Western hotel.

Only it'll be set in Kansas.   Ballads are for campfires, and their liars.
It won't tell you how I shot its subject
with a custom portrait
from Derringer Studios.

I only hope that since the song won't mention it
perhaps some day, a poet will –
that he was found with a sunflower
in his bottle of Hour Before.

Bucket of Blood

Larry D. Sweazy

Ashes and bricks
Sweat and lost
Dreams stain the
Boardwalk in dark
Gray seams under
Boot spurs and
Jingle, jangle, in
The pocket for
A day, night,
Or, two, with
The Virginia City
Ladies who favor
Rocky Mountain Punch
Champagne, rum, lemons
Sugar to sweeten
The trail smell
Where dreams die
Hard and winter
Never falls on
the restless cowboy.

After the Reviver

Jane Wheeler

He limped through my door on a Tuesday
ordered Laird's in a long stemmed glass,
his spurs etching scars in the floor boards,
he ponied up his bittersweet past.

His first ride was an old palomino,
his grandma taught him to rope
before billboards and highways demolished
what was left of the west's cowboy code.

He talked good colts and good women,
the bronc that shattered his hip,
cattle and ranches and weather,
then giving his Stetson a tip

he drank his last spot of brandy
said he needed to see to his horse,
laid a five on the bar for my trouble
and left me to clean up the Corpse.

Sucker Punched

Nancy Simmonds

His ranch house   weathered by the restless winds
     dried by ceaseless sun
             lists to the east.

Rain swollen books   burst
     from a crate on the back porch.

Broken scarecrow   waves
     from an overgrown garden topped with tumbleweed.

Wild grapes
       cling
         to a sagging fence.

Long grasses   wind blown   flat tops.

Yet

lemon colored flowers
bloom in a broken whiskey barrel.

The photograph of a woman in an apricot dress
is stuck with chewing gum
         to the wall above the kitchen wall switch.

She is standing next to a grinning cowboy
holding a pineapple in his dirt encrusted hands.

Grandpa and this unknown woman.

She is not my grandmother.

Chisholm Trail

Frederick Michaels

This Chisholm stretches 800 miles,
not worn into earth, but a man's soul.
It loops San Antonio and Abilene,
running brown hills and broad prairie,
broken by myriad streams and lakes.
It tests a cowpuncher's manhood,
driving a 2,500 longhorn steer herd
to payday at a Kansas railhead.

Cattle are bed by the Trinity river.
I lie quietly awake on a thin bedroll,
sole sentinel on overnight watch,
dazzled by the wide canopy of sky
arching across all of my horizons.
I pray nothing spooks these cattle,
not sound nor scent disturb sleep,
as I'm here alone on my last drive.

Days north of the Brazos and Waco,
our trail boss was suddenly bit
by a powerful thirst for rye whiskey
and is off now with all to Fort Worth's
famous White Elephant saloon.
I'm not a tea totalin' man mind you,
but straight whiskey's not to my taste.
I'd wait on a Corpse Reviver in Abilene!

"Yeah, that'll sure uncross your legs!"
I'm not a big time haunt of saloons,
but a tasty jolt now and then's okay.
The best Corpse Reviver I've had...
was at the Drover's Hotel in Abilene.
Yep, so when trail boss asked me
if I'd watch the herd I said "sure."
Didn't want rot gut whiskey anyhow.

Laying here watching the Texas sky,
I can almost taste that French brandy,
mixed with maraschino and bitters...
I'd like a trip to France someday,
maybe right after this last cattle drive.
I've some money saved in Abilene
and I'm sure not gettin' any younger.
Oh, I've traveled some, but France...
"Let's see, what other saloon drinks
beat the pants off straight rye whiskey?"
I had a Stone Fence in Galveston once.
Bourbon and cider... tasty, but strange.
Oh, there was this punch in St. Louis –
Champagne, rum, maraschino, lemons,
sugar – I think called 'Rocky Mountain'.
Wow, I remember that was a good time.

Cattle sound loud 'moos' several times.
"Whoa, settle down you dogies now."
I am quickly to my feet and listening.
My eyes search the wall of darkness
in all directions out from my campfire,
only to no avail and no further mooing.
No sound of hooves. No sound of danger.
My hand's on a Colt 1851 Navy Revolver.

"Damn twitchy critters" I mutter aloud.
Where was I – oh, St. Louis and punch.
It was the eve of the new year, 1866.
I'd just mustered out of the U. S. Cavalry
and was workin' my way back to Kansas.
In the Planters Hotel bar they had punch
made from Champagne and Jamaica rum,
served by this pretty young redheaded...

I get up to throw more wood on the fire.
It's black as pitch out there without a moon.
... this pretty young redheaded..? No, no!
Now you're embellishing this story, Fred.
The barkeep was a bald, swarthy gent
who didn't particularly like my greenbacks.
Anyway, the punch was dizzyingly delicious,
and I er... don't remember any redhead.

Morning'll be coming soon and I need sleep.
I wonder how early trail boss'll be back here,
those barrel boardin' hungovers in tow?
I just can't help but let loose a wry chuckle.
Well, it's still near 500 miles yet to Abilene.
They'll have plenty of saddle time to sober up.
I hoist my saddle blanket up to my shoulders,
my head on my saddle; my hand on my gun.

The Glorious Fourth
Tory V. Pearman

The fourth day was glorious:
a yard of flannel and a golden
slipper. After three whiskey daisies,
we tripped up to Old Chum's field,
teased the jersey cows behind the stone fence.
A yellow dog barked as the sun fizzed
golden behind a lone tree.

A maiden's kiss: Balaklava nectar, life-prolonger;
there were bells ringing from Cheyenne
to Manhattan. An hour before sunset,
a maiden's blush became a widow's kiss,
a Rocky Mountain gut-punch,
deep in the solar plexus--
no corpse reviver in sight.

Courting Stella

Meredith Trede

The first time he saw me I was out on McAdoo
jumping logs. He asked my uncle who
that woman was, my uncle said, *That's no woman,*
that's Stella. I was 13 or 14. I always liked
jumping logs. They set the logs up for the water
to run off the mountain. Dudley was up
from San Antonio with his brother. We were paying
high wages. Grandma was. She hired him
to work the cattle. He thought I was fearless.
Next time he saw me was about two years later.
My father wanted to go from cattle to sheep. Sheep are better
for making money. He had to put in new fencing.
You have to fence low to keep sheep in, so my father
hired Dudley to help him fence. That's when
I was back living with my father. He told me,
don't think you can do here like you did
at your grandmother's. You hang your clothes up.
Do like I say. I'd never taken orders from a man
before. It was Grandma told me what to do. He didn't
have to talk that way. It really bent me. I never
did like it when a man told me what to do.

64

Red Mountain Freeway

Mike Nierste

Driving into the sunset
in a convertible 5.0 L Mustang
sunbeams fall like spears of flame
urging me to head west
past that transmission line, across that horizon line
to live on that edge
or beyond
in the wild.

Oh
to grow
my handlebar mustache and hop on a Harley - growling
and turn my ear
to the whispers and howls of the earth
to drive into hundreds of sunset shreds of red
so they merge with my hundreds of hues of blues
till mountains majesty emerge - purple
to fly into a desert rain and only stop to smell the air filled with sweet
Greasewood and Mesquite when monsoon is complete
to raise my arm like a Saguaro cactus to say goodbye or hello to
conciliations
something, anything to rekindle the spirit of the unbroken
wild.

I watch one hundred hues of maiden's blush glowing and transforming
to shades of Indian paintbrush in wisps of clouds but rain refuses to fall.
I wait with skeleton buckwheat, leafless milkweed and palo verde for
monsoon to bring back signs of life.
Instead of driving to that edge, I return to the convenience and comforts
of home.
TexMex
washed down with widow's kisses
listening to rock and roll from a dobro guitar downloaded from the
internet - streaming
hot shower
clean shaven
turned downed sheets
down comforter
back to dreamland
with my head pointed
west.

Back Then

Margaret Britton Vaughn

Today men's socks come in
sizes 6 ½ - 9 and 9 – 13.
Back then, in the early fifties,
they broke down individually
in half and whole sizes.
Today men's socks come mostly in
black, blue, brown, and white;
back then, in the early fifties,
they were broke down in many colors.
Today men's socks are mostly cotton
back then, they were slick nylon.
Back then, if you were looking for me
during the Christmas Holidays,
you'd have found me broke down
behind a hill of mixed up socks
at Woolworth's Five and Dime sock counter.
It was nerve-racking keeping
socks straight in colors and sizes,
but more nerve-racking was the girl
at the record counter playing
my favorite cowboy singing
Rudolph the Red-nosed Reindeer
over and over and over for hours.
I wanted to scream out loud,
but no one would have heard me
because Rudolph was blaring
and I was buried in socks.
Too young to drink, I imagined jumping on old Grit,
riding her to an old cowboy watering hole,
swinging open those old batwing double doors,
walking up to the brass rail mirrored bar,
yelling, "Gimme a Yard of Flannel in all sizes,
put in lots of ale for my boiling - aching head
and leave out the nutmeg, for I'm already nuts."
Then, I would have headed Santa
off at the pass of socks,
tossed the flannel over Rudolph's nose,
handed old St. Nick a flashlight,
told Gene Autry to get off the record
and get back in the saddle again.
Oh Lord, a lady needs a pair of
7 ½ green socks for her son.
I'm sure there's a pair in there somewhere.

Transference

Alessio Zanelli

Cold sweat down hot temples.

Longing for a drop of *mezcal*,
either with or without worm,
sooner than a glass of water.

The whole place—
steep screes,
diving fissures
and pallid pinnacles—
shouts its enmity and scorn
at our shrunken guts.

Are we lost in the Sonoran Desert
or in the Canyon del Muerto?

Nah—this is just a Dolomite park.

Still,
at dusk,
when the gorge goes silent,
we can hear Cochise's
savage battle cry
at the blue jackets
or Ike Clanton's
mocking laughter
at the posse.

The Corpse Reviver

Steven Owen Shields

Ezekiel Ross made his living as a corpse reviver.
Nobody knew how he did it. He didn't know
himself. Somewhat like a water witch,
or Baptist preacher, he'd spread his gnarled and ruddy
hands in front of him, raise a rheumy
eye up to the clouds, beseeching God
(some said Satan) to deliver the deceased
from all his suffering and to *fetch him back!*

It was almost always a "him," by the way,
some drunken galoot who got hauled out
of some watering hole or shebang from playing
Faro when a sheriff would swing through the flimsy
doors to demand, *all right, which one of you*
piss-ants molested that apothecary's daughter?
And some joker would thickly tell the sheriff
to go back east and stick it, and that was all
it would take to see the two of them, drawn
revolvers at both ends of a rutted street,
one of them coughing up blood and cheap whisky.

And they'd take the dead cowman in a hand-cart
over to the town undertaker to be
"boxed up," (assuming his widow was willing
to pay for the service). The barber would helpfully offer
a cut-rate shave (*well, he sure ain't*
in no danger now, in case I cough)
and the words, *you know, ma'am, you could always*
call that corpse reviver feller and see
what HE could do! And the barber would laugh
and laugh, and slap his thigh, hack up a lung,
and the undertaker would break into a grin
because in thirty years, nobody had ever
seen anything of the sort.

                      Except this one time.
She was just a little girl, and Doc had tried
everything to save her but her blue eyes
finally closed. She lay silent in Momma's
upstairs bedroom, her long blonde hair
fanning a lacy pillow, cooling from fever.
And everyone below could hear her mother
weeping. One of them soon saddled up,
rode out hard to fetch back Ezekiel Ross.

And he arrived in cadaverous black, and the people
were silent as he entered the house. He held up his hand

68

and intoned them to "wait," so they did, on the porch,
while the morning sun glanced off the rain barrel,
the birds reducing themselves to silence. And he tramped
up the creaky stairs of the ancient boarding house,
asked the young mother to leave the room
until finally he and the girl were alone.

And he took her small hand and he held it, stroking
it tenderly, prayerfully—said a few soft words
and the little girl opened her eyes, and smiled weakly.
And he threw back the door without another word,
just smiled at the girl sitting upright and well,
trudged back down the creaky stairs as the sounds
of rejoicing streamed forth from the open windows
to the listening town. Then he mounted his horse and departed,
some said never to return, and drifted
away to the hills from whence he had come.
Nobody saw him again. Ezekiel Ross
made his living as a corpse reviver. Nobody knew
how he did it. He didn't quite know how himself.

Another Hour Before
Clyde Kessler

(time warping to the saloon to drink an hour before)

At sunset you watch the sky being saddled
by winter clouds. There's not one steer
on the ridge, just some creatures brushing
darkness fast against cactus thorns. There's
no song you want to remember to sing,
only a crazy dog yelping from the granary
as if it knows your jeep needs a jump start,
as if it's going to morph real into Sasquatch
and chase you to the saloon. You don't
need to be chased, of course. It's twenty
miles from nowhere, but you'll get there.

Wyoming

Katrina Hays

Change is the cruelest savior
                    -   Greg Glazner

In the dark outside the bar
Shouts and that woman's shrieking laugh
And the whump-whump of the bad band
Muffled by the mercy of a heavy door

I draw in breaths polluted by the grease trap
Fumble out a cigarette
Flame's brief heat fair penance
For inhaling my death

Snow bites through thin dancing boots
Such red vanities
Invisible Snow King sleeps above
Its solidity a rebuke

Do you follow me out to continue
Oh yes
Yellow Dogs and yearning carry you
Fists stuffed in a Carhartt jacket

I yank down my own Whiskey Daisy haze
But you deliver another electric prod
How that burning feels like grace
Your ring scorching my hand

Still the muffled music and winter stars
Do I snatch you by the throat
Yes I do
Stop words with a fist

Do I drop your body
Yes
Walk out of that alley to my truck
Wipe hands free of your tangle

Drive west until roads stop
and dreams fall down

Phantasms in the Sky (forgive me, Outlaws)

Thomas O'Dore

a drunk cowboy went riding out one hot and sunny day
dismounted by a *Stone Fence* and puked his guts away
when in the sky he saw a pie-dropping herd \ of *Jersey Cow(s)*
plodding past his blurry eyes \ harassed by a *Yellow Dog*

there ain't no waaay !... this can't be sooo !
hallucinations in the sky
their ear-tags were on fire and their steel udders clanked
like a *Manhattan Bell Ringer* on a *Glorious Fourth*

a bolt of *Rocky Mountain Punch* he heaved
as he saw the drovers \ double-vision in his eyes
there ain't no waaay !...this can't be sooo !
doppelgangers in the sky

their bloodshot eyes and a *Widow's Kiss* lipstick
was enough to cause \ a chaste *Maiden's Blush*
as they stumbled by he thought \ they'll never catch that herd
on any horse born of this earth \ and they're too drunk to try

there ain't no waaay !...this can't be sooo !
apparitions in the sky
as the horses wobbled by one rider cursed him out
"out the way you çoβ \ lest you need a *Corpse Reviver*"

"after you get trampled \ into *Balaclava Nectar*"
"just about an *Hour Before* \ it's bean time tonight"
there ain't no waaay !...this can't be sooo !

cowboys if you have too much rye
you too may see \ *phantasms in the sky*
phan...tas...ms !...innn !!... the skyyyy !!!

Directions From a Short Circuit

Garrett Flagg

Suddenly weak, teary-eyed for no reason, I lug
My carcass into a saloon. It is too much, I mutter, pointing
My gaze from the direction of blinding light.

The desert's fingers are thorns, her smile
An exotic hip dancing life, inviting me to the hurt,
The fragrant sashay of sacred pain.

I have been searching in all the crazy corners,
I tell her, but now I know this sun-drenched parch,
This sandy arroyo is where rain carved a river.

The wrong places are best, she tells me, *when digging*
Comes for treasure. It is like the tick's bite,
A skin disruption, a dimpled itch, fever.

You have scratched to madness, have you not?
Her question tells me what I have known too well.
Delirium and mirage sang me to sleep.

She loves my toothy grin, my ridiculous gasp at worlds
That make a quester rich with recognition.
But it was my shadow lit the fire and I, mere puppet.

What you feel, she says, holding my hand,
Is emptiness, perfect for this evening's festive dance.
Lithe, supple, bright as candles, she sways.

She pours me wine in a cup, a corpse reviver
Filled with ponies of brandy and maraschino,
Boker bitters dashed twice. A drink
Fit for gentlemen who pick on their scabs.

The dance holds me like a question for my motion
Is far from near, a spin at the periphery of desire.
My body heaves, a tomb lit with pepper and fire.

Cowpoke Cocktail

Timothy Robbins

All the world's a cocktail. Every man
and woman, all cattle and stallions,
traditions too — headiness of gin,
vermouth, cherries — you name it.
Cowboys and cowgirls are buckaroos
which are vaqueros, which were
Indians exploited by self-exiled
Spaniards who learned all they knew
from Moors who learned it from
Persians. The saloon at the end of the
powdery street sucking life in through
its clapping doors (were they really
like that?) and spitting it back out —
it's a cocktail as well. Sugary Miss
Kitty's Place on *Gunsmoke*. Spaghetti
Westerns flooded with bloody Marys.
The real thing, Wyatt Earp's The
Dexter made as unreal as 1960s
TV by time and popularity. The only
cowboy I ever met liked his drink
built on bitters stirred by stressful
work and strapping grace (these
aren't myths) and passion and love
and prejudice and not as much violence
as snowflakes fear or 50s kids with
chaps and spurs if their folks had
decent salaries believed and mimicked.
The piano player pounds out songs
on the dead notes alone. He
buys one whiskey sour per night
after which he drinks the potions
customers buy him. The whiskey
salesman from *Stage Coach* is a
teetotaling opium head. He watches
saloon doors like he watches
his heart's valves. Lassos are ropes
weaving cocktails of their bodies.
Saddles are shot glasses.

First Cow Town in Kansas

Linda Neal Reising

Chief Black Dog and the Osage
were the first to call the bluffs
of Baxter Springs home, but after
the war between brothers, cavalcades
of Texas cattlemen drove their herds
north to Kansas City, railroad link
to the East. Cowboys and other rowdies
poured into Baxter, first cattle town
in Kansas, brimming with stables,
brothels, saloons, where drovers
pounded dust from their hats and boots,
cleaned the creases of their faces
at the watering troughs before slapping
coins down on the counter for a whiskey—
raw alcohol with burnt sugar and a pinch
of tobacco—or a shot of rotgut, cut
by the barkeep with turpentine, gunpowder,
cayenne. A cocktail order drew the wrath
and sometimes pistols of local toughs
who left their games of Chuck-A-Luck
and Three-Card-Monte to jeer and poke
at the dandy, unless, of course, he happened
to be visiting Miss Nellie Starr at Wiggin's
House, where she plied her trade, plied
her customers with a Corpse Reviver—
maraschino bobbing like a plucked heart—
or a Maiden's Blush— the green anise
spirit of wormwood turned rosy
with raspberry syrup. And those passing
through never knew that The Life Prolonger,
with its sherry and port, did nothing to save
Marshal Henry the day he came to solve
a dispute between the lady of "ill-repute"
and one Isham Good, cowhand unhappy
with their arrangements. Both Nellie
and Isham drew, fired, leaving the marshal
mortally wounded, but only Good faced
the rope before posting bail and high-tailing
it south to Indian Territory, land of the Cherokee,
while Miss Nellie paid a fine for profane
discourse and boisterous talk, then returned
to her trade, perfecting, in honor of the marshal's
wife, a drink entitled the Widow's Kiss.

Stone Fence

Patrick T. Reardon

I built me a stone fence
by stacking one glass
of Maker's Mark whisky
on another,
interspersed with
large lumps of ice,
mortared with sweet cider.

I built me a stone fence
in a circle and,
when it was done,
leaped inside the circuit and
fell down the well to
the center of the Earth where
I met Buddha, Our Lady of Light,
the Queen of Clubs and
St. Augustine who wanted to
get on the wagon but
not just yet.

I built me a stone fence
across the face of northwest Ireland
as if to corral the island's
saints, fairies, snakes, nuns and travelers
in the backroom of a pub where
the constable is writing poetry,
and I long for coffee.

I built me a stone fence
and went out on Main Street
in noonday sun
where Johnny Raptor,
wanted in seven states,
called me out,
and, as I drew,
my skull was thundered with
a screaming headache that
no hangover remedy was ever going
to calm.

I built me a stone fence
and then crawled under the weight of it all
into my sympathetic grave.

One Thirsty Cowboy

Diane Jacks Saunders

The dusty trail makes a cowboy dry,
When he's herding cows all day.
I couldn't wait to get me a drink,
After I picked up my week's pay.

I heard about a new watering hole,
Called the True Grit Saloon.
Me and my pony ran to town,
I just had to get there soon.

I walked through the swinging doors,
And much to my surprise,
A big bright sign read "Jersey Cow,"
I couldn't believe my eyes!

Since when did a perfect watering hole,
Start cooking and serving up steaks?
What kind of beef cow is a Jersey?
This has got to be a mistake!

I knew all about Herefords and Angus,
And Longhorns and Charolais, too.
But a Jersey is a dairy cow,
Will a steak from a Jersey do?

I bellied up to the bar to order,
A rare steak and a mug of beer,
Barkeep says, "drinks only, cowboy,"
"What?" I says, "I didn't hear."

I pointed to the Jersey Cow sign,
And the Barkeep nods his skull.
"That's a popular drink here, cowboy,
"Just drink them till you're full."

"Just what's in that Jersey Cow," I asked.
"I want to be sure it's a dandy."
Barkeep says, "parfait de amaour,
"Maraschino and some apricot brandy."

So, I ordered me a Jersey Cow,
And it came with some cream on top.
Once I started drinking that quencher,
I discovered I couldn't stop.

Finally, I figured I'd had enough,
And staggered out to my horse,
I climbed up into my saddle,
He knew the way home, of course.

I'm glad to be herding the Angus,
The Jersey Cow didn't set well with me.
The True Grit Saloon is very nice,
But the dusty trail suits me to a T.

Shotgun Wedding Blues
Frank LP Kothbauer

Here I sit on the day I've dreaded,
About to wed that girl redheaded.
I will need me much more
Than an Hour Before
Of drinking until I'm lightheaded!

Hooch and Pooch: The Moonshine of Life

John Sherman

mere hours before
the glorious fourth
my yellow dog and I
scaled stone fences
so she could chase the jersey cows
grab three feet of flannel
for the blushing maiden
toss it around in the air
then drop it to run to the lone tree in the field
while I longed for the kiss of that daisy the neighboring widow

but the thought stirred up my solar plexus so much
I needed not one but two shots of balaklava nectar
preferably at my favorite watering hole with the cowboys of amarillo
to revive this old chum and prolong my life
but instead I visited the nearby golden slipper saloon in tombstone
where the former manhattan bell-ringer
now served whiskey shaken to a golden fizz
learned from a benefactor who built the saloon
to replicate one he'd owned in the wild rocky hills back east

alas: the nectar the fizz and
the whiskey nearly made me a corpse
but with glee and a smile and a kiss blown to all
I swore off drink

until temptation revived me
and I leaned in and reached for my next shot
from my reclaimed bar stool

last chance saloon
RC deWinter

all the cowboys fresh in off the range jostlin' three deep at the bar
are drunk
achin' between the legs and lookin' for
someone to worship for the night and
somewhere there's a tinny player piano tinklin' through old chestnuts

you are my sunshine in the good old summertime

but there's no sunshine here
only cigar smoke clouds in a kerosene sky
there's not much good about it
it's not even summer

some of the drunker buffalo gals are howlin' along
out of tune out of time makin' eyes
at the greenhorns just off the last stage
while out back old man river is gettin' fresh with darlin' clementine

and the sheriff's lookin' the other way
'cause clemmie turned him down
so she deserves what she gets

i don't belong here
it's not my time it's not my place
what swindled me into this wild west nightmare
of every shallow cliché you can think of?

it must be a dream
there's a queer ache in my chest
and though i keep lookin' for the door
i can't seem to find it

now the bartender's pourin' another yellow dog
and sendin' me a nasty smile and
oh shit!
his teeth are pointed and so are his ears
oh let me wake up

Heartbreak Heroine

S. K. Naus

Jessie Jane is her name
She has clout, she has fame
Absinthe green are her eyes
Raspberry lips tell no lies
And her Colt 45
Is what keeps her alive.
She comes into town
Wearing trousers not a gown
On a horse black as night
Ready for a fight.
She's not sugar and spice
Nor all things nice
She's angry, she's mad
She'll hurt someone bad.
Wild Bill stole her heart
And stabbed it with a dart
Took her money and ran
Jessie Jane will find that man.
Her maiden's blush long gone
Since love went all wrong
Her rage is more hateful
And life more fateful.
The saloon is full and loud
At the bar stands a crowd
Wild Bill buying drinks
For all friends and finks.
Jessie Jane bursts in
Her gun pointed at him
People scatter and run
The evening's lost its fun.
"Give me my money,
And don't call me Honey."
She screams at Wild Bill
So ready to kill.
He gulps back his gin
And gives her a grin
To win back her heart
And make a new start.
"I won't fall for that
So give it all back!"
Wild Bill holds up his hands
But remains where he stands.

80

"I will not fight you.
Nothing you can do."
Everyone is staring
She does not lose her bearing.
She remembers his horse
With saddle bags, of course
Tied up next to hers
So she jingles her spurs.
The money's stashed there
And snatch it she'll dare.
In a flash, she is gone
Gun no longer drawn
On his horse, she rides west
To the sunset for rest.

Horse Speaking to Rider

Bill Ayres

Because I am broken,
I let you nail on new iron
when shoes comes loose from my hooves.

I don't fight when you back me into the trailer.
I eat your dry hay. I wait
too long for someone to muck out my stall.

Though it gags me,
I stand still when you put the bit in my mouth.

Because I am broken,
I let you bridle and saddle me.
I accept leather straps
as part of me as I accept you
--your weight shifting above me,
the reins pulling my neck right and left
or straight back to get me to stop.

As much as it scares me,
I go where you want.
I jump fences I am not sure I can clear.
I race and take the blame
if I am too slow
or if I stumble.
When I was wild
there was nothing to chase me
to make me run like this.

Sweet is the apple you slice
and hold out on the flat of your palm.
And the way you take time to stroke my back and sides,
brushing me down, that is sweet.
Best of all are your knees tight against me
when you've had a few Yellow Dogs
after the cattle drive,
your heels in my flanks urging me on
as I gallop faster, faster, faster.

The Hour Before

Caitlin Cacciatore

THE HOUR BEFORE was spent quite
unlike any hour which had come before –
high noon was approaching with the patience of a sundial,
but our cowboy in his leather vest
was drinking a CORPSE REVIVER
not with the forlorn hope
of it helping him in the afterlife,
but rather in the interest
of making the MAIDEN'S BLUSH
look redder than a raspberry,
giving her lips the allure
of overripe cherries
as he licked the rouge
right off her lips.

the WIDOW'S KISS came next,
the poor woman weeping like a willow
over that which had yet to be lost,
and finally came the soggy embrace of a YELLOW DOG,
who had forgiven the man everything,
including being left out in the rain the night before –
and our cowboy took a long dreg of his LIFE-PROLONGER,
staggered out into the sunlight
just as the clocks were striking twelve,
wove his way into a passing duel,
and straight into an early grave.

Authentic Cowboy Cocktails

which might be found at the True Grit Saloon

Corpse Reviver
1 pony brandy
1 pony maraschino
2 dashes boker bitters
Place the above in a wine glass and serve.
The Gentleman's Table Guide, 1873

The Glorious Fourth
1 pony brandy
1 dash Jamaican rum
4 dashes gum syrup
1 large tablespoon ice cream
Juice of a lime
Add the above to a mixing glass two thirds full or ice. Shake this exceedingly well, strain into a fancy glass and serve.
The Flowing Bowl, 1892

Hour Before
1 wine glass sherry or madeira
1 dash Bokers or Angostura bitters
Add the above to a mixing glass, stir and serve in a glass.
Cooling Cups and Dainty Drinks, 1869

Maiden's Blush
½ wine glass old tom gin
½ teaspoon absinthe
1 teaspoon raspberry syrup
½ teaspoon powdered sugar
1 lemon
Fill a tumbler with chopped ice, add the sugar & syrup, and squeeze in half a lemon. Add the absinthe and gin, shake well, and strain into a colored glass. Serve with a slice of lemon on top.
American and Other Drinks, 1887

84

Old Chum's Reviver

½ wine glass brandy
1 liqueur glass strawberry syrup
Juice of ½ lemon
½ teaspoon sugar
Soda water

Fill a half-pint tumbler with chipped ice and add the juice, sugar, syrup, and brandy. Fill with soda water, shake well, ornament with fruit in season and serve with straws.
American and Other Drinks, 1887

Stone Fence

1 wine glass bourbon whiskey
Sweet cider

Add the whiskey and two or three lumps of ice to a large bar glass. Fill the glass with sweet cider and serve.
The Bon-Vivant's Companion, 1862

Widow's Kiss

1 pony apple brandy
½ pony yellow chartreuse
½ pony Benedictine
2 dashes angostura bitters

Add the above to a mixing glass half full of fine ice, shake well, strain into a fancy cocktail glass, and serve.
Modern American Drinks, 1895

Yellow Dog

½ cocktail glass scotch whiskey
½ cocktail glass vermouth
1 orange

Place in mixing glass filled with ice, shake well, and strain into a bar glass. Add a small piece of orange peel.
Louis' Mixed Drinks, 1906

Lone Tree Cocktail

2 liqueur glasses dry gin
1 liqueur glass french vermouth
2 dashes maraschino
Fill a mixing glass with ice, add the above ingredients, stir well, and strain into a cocktail glass. Twist a small piece of lemon peel on top and add the peel to the cocktail.
Louis' Mixed Drinks, 1906

Jersey Cow

1/3 parait de amour
1/3 maraschino
1/3 apricot brandy
Pour carefully in a liqueur glass equal amounts of the above cordials. Float a little cream on top.
Louis' Mixed Drinks, 1906

Whiskey Daisy No. 3

1 wine glass whiskey
2 teaspoons pineapple syrup
2 teaspoons lemon juice
1 teaspoon powdered sugar
Fill a mixing glass two-thirds full of fine ice. Add the above ingredients, shake well, strain into a cocktail glass, fill with carbonated water, and serve.
How to Mix Drinks, 1904

Balaklava Nectar

(for a party of 15)

2 bottles Claret

1 bottle champagne

2 bottles soda water

2 tablespoons powdered sugar

3 lemons

½ small cucumber

Peel and shred fine the rind of half a lemon and cut the cucumber into fine slices leaving the peel on. Place these in a punch bowl and add the sugar and the juice of both lemons. Toss it up several times and add the claret, champagne, and soda water. Stir well and serve.

(Balaklava, a seaport on the Black Sea in southwest Soviet Russia, was the scene of the charge of the Light Brigade during the Crimean War in 1854.)

Bar-Tender's Guide, 1887

Rocky Mountain Punch

5 bottles Champagne

1 quart Jamaica rum

1 pint maraschino

6 slice lemons

Sugar to taste

This delicious punch is compounded as follows. Mix the above ingredients in a large punch bowl and then place in the center of the bowl a large square block of ice. Ornament it with rock candy, loaf sugar, sliced lemons or oranges and fruits in season. This is a splendid punch for New Year's Day.

The Bon-Vivant's Companion, 1862

Golden Slipper

(Use a wine glass)

½ Yellow Chartreuse

1 egg yolk

½ Danziger Goldwasser

Don't let the yolk of the egg run into the liqueurs.

U.S. Bartender's Guide, 1891

A Maiden's Kiss
1/5 Maraschino
1/5 Crème de Roses
1/5 White Curacao
1/5 Yellow Chartreuse
1/5 Benedictine
Fill a sherry glass with the above. Keep each layer separate
The Flowing Bowl, 1892

Golden Fizz
1 wine glass Old Tom Gin (or whiskey)
1 egg yolk
3 dashes lemon or lime juice
1 tablespoon fine white sugar
Place the above ingredients in a large bar glass with two or three small lumps of ice, shake thoroughly, strain into a medium bar glass, and fill with seltzer water.
Bar-Tender's Guide, 1887

Manhattan Bell-Ringer
½ wine glass bourbon whiskey
½ wine glass vermouth
½ teaspoon Abricotine
1 Dash Peychaud or Angostura bitters
2 dashes orange bitters
2 teaspoons gum syrup
½ teaspoon lemon juice
Fill mixing glass 2/3 full of fine ice. Add bourbon whiskey, vermouth, bitters, lemon juice, and syrup and stir thoroughly. Put one-half teaspoon of Abricotine into the cocktail glass, rinse it so that the Abricotine will be evenly coated all over inside of the glass, then strain the mixture into it and serve.
How to Mix Drinks, 1904

Yard of Flannel

1 Quart Ale
6 Eggs
4 Tablespoons Brown Sugar
A Little Nutmeg

Put a quart of ale in a tinned saucepan on the fire to boil; in the meantime, beat u the yolks of 4 eggs with the whites of 2 eggs, adding four tablespoons of brown sugar and a little nutmeg. Pour the egg mixture on the ale by degrees, beating so as to prevent the mixture from curling. Then pour back and forward repeatedly from vessel to vessel, raising the hand to a great a height as possible, which process produces the smoothness and frothing essential to the good quality of the drink. This is excellent for a cold and from its fleecy appearance, is designated "a yard of flannel." It is also known as an egg flip.
The Bon-Vivant's Companion, 1862

Solar Plexus

2/3 Wine Glass Bourbon Whiskey
½ Teaspoon Abricotine
1 Teaspoon Lemon Juice
1 Teaspoon Gum Syrup
1 Pony Unfermented Grape Juice
1 Piece of Sliced Pineapple
Seltzer

Place the above in an old-fashioned cocktail glass, dash with seltzer, stir with a spoon, and serve.
How to Mix Drinks, 1904

The Life-Prolonger

2/3 Pony Sherry Wine
1/3 Pony Port Wine
2 Ponies Cream
1 Fresh Egg
1 Spoon Fine Sugar

Add the above to a mixing glass and shake exceedingly well. Strain into a large glass and serve.
The Flowing Bowl, 1892

Hot Benefactor

2/3 Pony Jamaica Rum
1 1/3 Ponies Chianti
1 Slice Lemon
2 or 3 Lumps Sugar
A Little Nutmeg

Dissolve two or three lumps of sugar in a large hot punch glass filled with one pony of boiling water. Add one-and-one-third ponies of Chianti, two-thirds pony of Jamaica rum and one slice of lemon. Grate a little nutmeg on top and serve.

The Flowing Bowl, 1892

Editor

Barry Harris is editor of the *Tipton Poetry Journal* and two other anthologies by Brick Street Poetry: *Mapping the Muse: A Bicentennial Look at Indiana Poetry* and *Words and Other Wild Things.* He has published one poetry collection, *Something At The Center.* Barry lives in Brownsburg, Indiana and is retired from Eli Lilly and Company. His poetry has appeared in *Kentucky Review, Valparaiso Poetry Review, Grey Sparrow, Silk Road Review, Saint Ann's Review* and *Flying Island.* One of his poems was on display at the National Museum of Sport and another is painted on a barn in Boone County, Indiana as part of Brick Street Poetry's Word Hunger public art project.

Contributor Biographies

David Alpaugh has published more than 200 poems, essays, and plays in journals that include *Able Muse, American Journal of Poetry, Chronicle of Higher Education, Evergreen Review, Exquisite Corpse, Gargoyle, Light, Mudlark, Poetry, Rattle, Scene4, Spillway, X-Peri,* and *Zyzzyva*. His poetry is included in the Dana Gioia anthology *California Poetry from the Gold Rush to the Present* and he has been a finalist for Poet Laureate of California. He teaches for the Osher Lifelong Learning Institute at its U.C. Berkeley and Cal State East Bay campuses.

Bill Ayres lives in Virginia and comes from a long line of rustlers. So far he's managed not to get hanged. His poems have appeared lately in *Commonweal, Hoot, The Roanoke Review*....

Joe Bisicchia writes of our shared dynamic. An Honorable Mention recipient for the Fernando Rielo XXXII World Prize for Mystical Poetry, his works have appeared in numerous publications. He lives in New Jersey and his website is www.JoeBisicchia.com.

Vienna Bottomley was born and raised in the Indianapolis area. She is a "triple domer" who earned B.A. and M.A. degrees in English from the University of Notre Dame and will graduate with her J.D. from Notre Dame Law School in 2019. She lives with her husband, Adrian, and Cooper, the original yellow dog.

Shirley J. Brewer graduated from careers in bartending, palm-reading and speech therapy. She serves as poet-in-residence at Carver Center for Arts & Technology in Baltimore, Maryland. Recent poems garnish *Barrow Street, Chiron Review, Comstock Review, Poetry East, Slant,* and other journals. Shirley's poetry books include *A Little Breast Music* (2008, Passager Books), *After Words* (2013, Apprentice House) and *Bistro in Another Realm* (2017, Main Street Rag). www.apoeticlicense.com

Michael Brockley is a 68-year old, newly retired school psychologist who worked for 31 years in rural northeast Indiana. Recent poems have appeared in *Atticus Review, Gargoyle* and *Jokes Review.*

Melanie Browne is a poet and fiction writer from Texas. Her writing has appeared in many online journals and a few anthologies. A former art teacher, she has written two chapbooks, *Heaven is a Giant Pawn Shop* and *Portrait of a Bad sailor Girl.*

Caitlin Cacciatore is a New York City-based poet, writer, and dreamer. She sees beauty in both everyday mundanities and in the profound experiences life has to offer. Her work is reflective of a deep and enduring love for the English language, as well as a vivid imagination and a certain 'joie de vivre.'

John Irvin Cardwell is a contemporary writer of poems, stories and essays who was raised on an Indiana farm that he still owns and manages with his wife Nancy Griffin. John's books include *The Good Road Home* and *Dances in a West African Night*, and two new volumes scheduled for publication in 2019 or 2020. John is a great grandfather, a former teacher in Indiana and Nigeria, and a long time public policy advocate who has had poems published in the *Tipton Poetry Journal* and elsewhere.

Joan Colby has published widely in journals such as *Poetry, Atlanta Review, South Dakota Review, Gargoyle, Pinyon, Little Patuxent Review, Spillway, Midwestern Gothic* and others. Awards include two Illinois Arts Council Literary Awards and an Illinois Arts Council Fellowship in Literature. She has published 21 books including Selected Poems from FutureCycle Press which received the 2013 FutureCycle Prize and Ribcage from Glass Lyre Press which has been awarded the 2015 Kithara Book Prize. Three of her poems have been featured on Verse Daily and another is among the winners of the 2016 Atlanta Review International Poetry Contest. Her newest books are *Carnival from FutureCycle Press, The Seven Heavenly Virtues* from Kelsay Books, *Her Heartsongs* from Presa Press and *Joyriding to Nightfall* from Futurecycle Press.   Colby is a senior editor of *FutureCycle Press* and an associate editor of *Good Works Review*. Website: www.joancolby.com. Facebook: Joan Colby. Twitter: poetjm.

Eli Cleary lives in Connecticut and works as a Programs Director in IT. Her poetry has been published in numerous journals and anthologies across the country including *Tipton Poetry Journal, Off the Coast, Blood and Thunder*, and *Vermont Literary Review*. She is not a cowboy but does ride horses and enjoys cocktails, albeit not at the same time. Her dog's name is Riley and her new favorite drink is Stone Fence.

Justice M. Cundiff is a writer and graduate student from central Kentucky. She is a young woman who loves nothing more than reading, writing, and warm coffee on cold mornings.

RC deWinter is a superannuated debutante who writes in many genres but has been focusing on poetry for some time now. Her only claim to fame is a decent Twitter following. Nevertheless, her poetry is anthologized in *Cowboys & Cocktails, Poetry from the True Grit Saloon,* (Brick Street Poetry, 2019), *New York City Haiku* (NY Times, 2017), *Uno: A Poetry Anthology* (Verian Thomas, 2002), in print in *2River View, Meat For Tea: The Valley Review, Pink Panther Magazine, Down in the Dirt, Scarlet Leaf Review, Genre Urban* Arts and featured in numerous online journals.

Christine Donat is senior at SUNY New Paltz who is passionate about reading and creative writing. She finds inspiration through self-analysis and the psyche, and through exploring the wonderful literature that surrounds that world.

Rosanne Ehrlich's novel *Attack* was published by Ballantine Books under the pen name Collis Ehrlich. Flash pieces have been published in *Persimmon Tree* and *Panoply. Fredericksburg Literary and Art Review* has published four of her poems, a short non-fiction piece has been published in *Metafore Magazine* and a fiction piece in *Antirrhinum Journal.* She has also written several television documentaries for *The Great Ships* series on *The History Channel.*

After graduating from De la Salle College in Manila, **Garrett Flagg** earned degrees in Communications and English, and taught at community colleges in Texas and North Carolina and retired in 2015. He has published poems in *Sky Islands, Nightsun, McGuffin, Cream City Review, Quixote Quarterly, The Greensboro Review*, etc. He does photography, paints, draws, plays pickleball, and maintains a Facebook website, *Why Write.*

Cowboys & Cocktails: Poetry from the True Grit Saloon

Maureen Tolman Flannery, who grew up on a sheep and cattle ranch in Wyoming, is an English teacher, wood-carver and Home Funeral Guide. Her nine books of poetry include *Ancestors in the Landscape, Following the Cabin Home,* and *Tunnel into Morning.*

Merlin Flower is an independent artist and writer in India. On twitter: @merlinflower.

Rosemary Freedman is a poet, a painter and an advanced practice nurse. She has 7 children and lives in Carmel, Indiana with her husband Jack. Rosemary enjoys growing peonies and tending her large garden. She is a graduate of Indiana University.

Katrina Hays was a river guide (in Jackson, Wyoming among other places) before finding her way to writing. Work has appeared in *Flash Fiction Magazine, WomenArts Quarterly, Psychological Perspectives, Bellingham Review, Apalachee Review,* and *Crab Creek Review,* with poems forthcoming in *The Hollins Critic.* She lives in Oregon and is on the guest faculty of the Rainier Writing Workshop at Pacific Lutheran University, where she received an MFA in Creative Writing.

Joseph Heithaus lives a true, but not so gritty life in Greencastle, Indiana where he teaches at DePauw University. His writing has appeared in many places including the *New York Times,* the *Southwest Review,* and the *Tipton Poetry Journal* as well as on a window in the Indianapolis airport and on the side of a local barn. He has written the book *Poison Sonnets* and co-authored *Rivers, Rails, and Runways* and *Airmail.*

Alexis Ivy is a 2018 recipient of the Massachusetts Cultural Council Fellowship in Poetry. Her first poetry collection, *Romance with Small-Time Crooks* was published in 2013 by BlazeVOX [books], and her second collection, *Taking the Homeless Census* won the 2018 Editors Prize at Saturnalia Books and is forthcoming in 2020. She is a Street Outreach Advocate working with the homeless and lives in her hometown, Boston.

Michael Keshigian, from New Hampshire, will have his thirteenth poetry collection, *The Garden Of Summer* released this Spring, 2019 by Flutter Press. He has been widely published in numerous national and international journals, recently including *Red River Review, Wild Violet Magazine, Bluepepper, Muddy River Review, Smoky Quartz* and has appeared as feature writer in over twenty publications with 6 Pushcart Prize and 2 Best Of The Net nominations. (michaelkeshigian.com)

Clyde Kessler, of Radford, Virginia has had poems published in many magazines, most recently in *South Florida Poetry Journal, Still the Journal* and *Visitant.* In 2017 Cedar Creek published his book *Fiddling At Midnight's Farmhouse*, which his wife Kendall illustrated.

Connie Kingman, lifetime resident of Rensselaer, Indiana, is founder of Prairie Writers Guild and is a garden and nature writer.

Cowboys & Cocktails: Poetry from the True Grit Saloon

Terry Kirts is the author of *To the Refrigerator Gods,* which was chosen for the Editor's Choice series in poetry by Seven Kitchens Press in 2010. He is a senior lecturer in creative writing at Indiana University-Purdue University in Indianapolis. His poems, essays, and culinary articles appear widely, and he is a contributing editor for food at *Indianapolis Monthly.*

Frank LP Kothbauer lives in Michigan and is – By day: a process control engineering leader and devoted family man. By night: a cheese curd connoisseur, craft beer enthusiast, and accomplished punner / limerickist.

Elizabeth Krajeck, Indianapolis, originally from Cavalier County, North Dakota, is the author of two chapbooks, including *TRIGGER.* Krajeck is recognized for her collaborations with visual artists, galleries, nonprofits and recently with the Quilt Connection Guild. She is a recipient of a Creative Renewal Fellowship from the Arts Council of Indianapolis and an Individual Artist Award from the Indiana Arts Commission. She is a community-based writer affiliated with Butler University's Center for Citizenship and Community.

Former Indiana Poet Laurate **Norbert Krapf** is the author of twelve poetry collections the latest of which is *The Return of Sunshine,* about his Colombian-German-American grandson who lives in Germany. He is the winner of a Glick Indiana Author Award, a Creative Renewal Fellowship from the Arts Council of Indianapolis, and the Lucille Memorial Award from the Poetry Society of America. He collaborates with bluesman Gordon Bonham and his play adaptation of his *Catholic Boy Blues* poetry collection is being performed in June, 2019 through IndyFringe.

Carolyn Kreiter-Foronda, Virginia Poet Laureate Emerita, has co-edited three anthologies and published eight poetry books, including *These Flecks of Color: New and Selected Poems* and *The Embrace: Diego Rivera and Frida Kahlo,* winner of the Art in Literature: Mary Lynn Kotz Award. Her poems appear in journals, such as *Nimrod, Prairie Schooner, Mid-American Review, World Poetry*

Doris Lynch has recent work in *Tipton Poetry Journal* as well as *frogpond, Flying Island, Haibun Today,* and the *Atlanta Review.* She won three Indiana individual artist's grants, and in 2017, she won the Genjuan International Haibun Award. She currently resides in Bloomington, Indiana.

Bonnie Maurer grew up in Indy, but inhabited Dodge City in those *Gunsmoke* nights when she watched the Western drama series on TV. Although she didn't dress like the sassy saloon keeper, Kitty, she loved to wear the cowgirl outfit her mother bought—the blue skirt and silver vest with white plastic fringe.

Kyla McDaniel is a resident of Zionsville, Indiana living with her husband Greg and daughters Stella and Lola. Kyla has her master's degree in Elementary Education. She currently teaches first grade at Stonegate Elementary School. Kyla has recently published her first poetry book titled *Between Moonbeams,* which is a combination of free verse poems and black out poetry.

Robin Michel's poetry and fiction has appeared in *Bird's Thumb, San Pedro River Review,* and elsewhere. Born in Salt Lake City, she now lives in San Francisco. Before his death, her father owned a bar in Paradise, California, a true grit town. After the 2018 Camp Fire, that building still stands.

Frederick Michaels was a metallurgist in a previous life, but now lives as a poet cowpoke in Indiana. His musings are found in trail gazettes and dusty bookstores. If you have an inkling, you can round up his book, *Potholes in the Universe*, from your local book peddler, Sam Amazon.

Marlene Million is a member of Noble Poets, Poetry Society of Indiana, National Fed. of State Poetry Societies,Inc. She has been published in: *The Polk Street Review, Tipton Poetry Journal*, several books and anthologies. She is currently working on a chapbook of her poetry.

Cheryl Soden Moreland is a Hoosier writer who embraces her Cherokee heritage and early childhood life on a southern reservation. She is the author of *Kokomo Kid ~ Reflections of Growing Up in Indiana's City of Firsts* (with Kokomo Kid ~ The Sequel coming out in 2019) as well as having essays published in *Urban Tapestry ~ Indianapolis Stories* and in *Undeniably Indiana*, with poetry in *And Know This Place ~ Poetry of Indiana*, along with several issues of *Tipton Poetry Journal*.

Lylanne Musselman is an award-winning poet, playwright, and artist, living in Indiana. Her work has appeared in *Pank, Flying Island, Tipton Poetry Journal, The New Verse News, and Ekphrastic Review,* among others, and many anthologies. Musselman is the author of five chapbooks, a co-authored volume of poetry, *Company of Women New and Selected Poems*, and a full-length poetry collection, *It's Not Love, Unfortunately* (Chatter House Press, 2018).

S.K. Naus lives in Ontario, has enjoyed writing since grade school and likes to enter contests on a lark. Words are important and arranging them in the right order can create wonderful stories.

J. Nguyen is a playwright, electronic musician, and writer living in Brooklyn. Nguyen has been published previously in *Tipton Poetry Journal, Open Thought Vortex, Sisyphus Quarterly, Crab Fat Magazine,* and *The Sex Letters Project;* Nguyen has also performed and written for The Boston Center for the Arts, The Living Gallery, Bindlestiff Studios, The Exponential Festival, and The Trans Theatre Festival.

Mike Nierste has been published in *Flying Island and frogpond.* Author of two chapbooks of poetry and a collection of quotations called *Contra-Diction.* Mike currently lives in Zionsville, Indiana.

Guys like **Tom O'Dore** do not have biographies.

Thomas Alan Orr writes and raises Flemish Giant rabbits in Shelby County, Indiana. Much of his work focuses on people who live close to the land and struggle to preserve Indiana 's agrarian spirit. He has published recently in the *Merton Seasonal* and *Flying Island.* He is a two-time Pushcart Prize nominee. His most recent collection is *Tongue to the Anvil: New and Selected Poems* (Restoration Press, 2014).

Tory V. Pearman is an Associate Professor of English at Miami Hamilton University, where she teaches composition and literature. She has published poetry in *San Pedro River Review, Atticus Review, Old Northwest Review, Tipton Poetry Journal,* and *Heartland Review* as well as essays on poetry, medieval literature, and disability studies.

96

Joseph S. Pete is an award-winning journalist, an Iraq War veteran, an Indiana University graduate, a book reviewer, a photographer, and a frequent guest on Lakeshore Public Radio. He is a Pushcart Prize and Best of the Net nominee who was named the poet laureate of Chicago BaconFest, a feat that Geoffrey Chaucer chump never accomplished. His writing and photography have appeared in more than 150 literary journals, including *Tipton Poetry Journal, Words and other Wild Things, Dogzplot, Stoneboat, The High Window, Synesthesia Literary Journal, Steep Street Journal, Beautiful Losers, New Pop Lit, The Grief Diaries, Gravel, The Offbeat, Oddball Magazine, The Perch Magazine, Rising Phoenix Review, Chicago Literati, Bull Men's Fiction, shufPoetry, The Roaring Muse, Prairie Winds, Blue Collar Review, Lumpen, The Rat's Ass Review, Euphemism, Jenny Magazine, Vending Machine Press* and *McSweeney's Internet Tendency*.Like Bartleby, he would prefer not to.

Kenneth Pobo has a new book out from Clare Songbirds Publishing House called *The Antlantis Hit Parade*. Forthcoming from Duck Lake Books is *Dindi Expecting Snow*. He teaches at Widener University in Pennsylvania.

Patrick T. Reardon is the author of eight books, including *Requiem for David*, a poetry collection from Silver Birch Press, and *Faith Stripped to Its Essence*, a literary-religious analysis of Shusaku Endo's novel *Silence*. Reardon, a former reporter with the Chicago Tribune, has had poetry published by *Silver Birch Press, Cold Noon, Eclectica, Esthetic Apostle, Ground Fresh Thursday, Literary Orphans, Rhino, Spank the Carp, Time for Singing, Tipton Poetry Journal, Under a Warm Green Linden* and *The Write City*. His poems have been nominated for a Pushcart Prize in 2016 and 2017. His novella *Babe* was short-listed by Stewart O'Nan for the annual Faulkner-Wisdom Contest of the Faulkner Society. His *Pump Don't Work* blog can be found at http://www.patricktreardon.com/blog/.

Linda Neal Reising, a native of Oklahoma and a member of the Western Cherokee Nation, has been published in numerous journals, including *The Southern Indiana Review, Nimrod,* and *Comstock Review.* Linda's poems and fiction have also been included in a number of anthologies, including *And Know This Place: Poetry of Indiana* and *Lost on Route 66: Tales of the Mother Road.* She was named the winner of the 2012 Writer's Digest Poetry Award, a finalist for the 2015 Oklahoma Book Award, winner of the 2015 Oklahoma Writers' Federation Poetry Book Prize, and nominee for a 2018 Pushcart Prize.

Stephen R. Roberts collects books, gargoyles, poetic lariats, and various other obstacles that fit into his basic perceptions of a chaotic and twisted world that pays scant attention to him as far as he knows. He's been published in *Alembic, Briar Cliff Review, Borderlands, Willow Springs, Karamu, Water-Stone, Bryant Literary Review, Yalobusha Review,* and many others. His full length collection, *Almost Music From Between Places*, is available from Chatter House Press. Stephen lives in Westfield, Indiana.

Timothy Robbins' poems have appeared in *Main Street Rag, Off The Coast, Bayou Magazine, Slant, Tipton Review* and many others. He has published three volumes of poetry: *Three New Poets (Hanging Loose Press), Denny's Arbor Vitae (Adelaide Books)* and *Carrying Bodies (Main Street Rag Press)*. He lives in Wisconsin with his husband of twenty-one years.

Diane Jacks Saunders is a retired newspaper reporter and photographer living in Indiana. She is also the author of *Our Ponies, My Cowboy and Me*, a book of cowboy poetry, and *Grace Street*, a biographical book about growing up in an ethnic neighborhood in the 1950s.

Mary Sexson is the author of *103 in the Light, Selected Poems 1996-2000 (Restoration Press)*, and co-author of *Company of Women, New and Selected Poems* (Chatter House Press). Her poetry has appeared in Flying Island, Tipton Poetry Journal, Hoosier Lit, New Verse News, and others, and several anthologies, including *Reckless Writing* (2013), *A Few Good Words* (2013), *The Best of Flying Island* (2015), and *Words and Other Wild Things* (2016). Her newest work is in Flying Island (2019) and Tipton Poetry Journal (2019). She was part of the Da Vinci Pursuit, a poetry project at Prophetstown State Park. Find her at **Poetry Sisters**, on Facebook.

John Sherman lives in Indianapolis and has published three poetry books, two spoken-word CDs, and nearly 100 poems in magazines and anthologies. Thanks, in part, to grants from the Indiana Arts Commission, he often provides poetry workshops for youth and adults.

Steven Owen Shields is a former all-night disc jockey from Indianapolis and present-day college professor of mass communication at the University of North Georgia. His second collection,*Creation Story*, has just been published by Brick Road Poetry Press of Columbus, Georgia.

On the Executive Committee for the Poetry Society of Indiana , **Nancy Simmonds** writes from Fort Wayne. Her worn and sassy cowgirl boots are a writer's inspiration. So are her athletic shoes. Nancy is on Amerithon mile 1498 of her virtual run/bike/swim across America.

Claude Clayton Smith, professor emeritus of English at Ohio Northern University, is the author of eight books and co-editor/translator of two others. His own work has been translated into five languages, including Russian and Chinese. For further information, please see his website: claudeclaytonsmith.wordpress.com.

Laurel Smith lives and writes in Vincennes, Indiana. Now retired from Vincennes University, Smith continues to advocate for education and the arts. Her poetry has appeared in various periodicals, including *Natural Bridge, New Millennium Writings, Tipton Review, English Journal, JAMA: Journal of the AMA;* also in the following anthologies: *And Know This Place, Visiting Frost,* and *Mapping the Muse.*

Larry D. Sweazy is the author of fourteen novels, and the winner of six national writing awards, including the WWA (Western Writers of America) Spur Award, the Will Rogers Medallion Award, and the Elmer Kelton Book Award. His poetry has appeared in the *Raintree Review*, the *Red River Review*, and the *Tipton Poetry Journal*. He lives in Noblesville, Indiana with his wife Rose, and is hard at work on his next novel.

Cowboys & Cocktails: Poetry from the True Grit Saloon

Meredith Trede's *Tenement Threnody* (persona poems in voices from her city childhood) is from Main Street Rag Press (2016). Stephen F. Austin State University Press published *Field Theory* (2011). A Toadlily Press founder, her chapbook, *Out of the Book,* was in *Desire Path.* Other journal publications include *Barrow Street, Cortland Review, Friends Journal, Witness,* and *Paris Review.* She was granted fellowships at Blue Mountain Center, Ragdale, Saltonstall, and the Virginia Center for the Creative Arts in Virginia and France, the Nicholson Political Poetry Award, and a NYFA travel grant. Meredith lives in New York. More information can be found at http://meredithtrede.com

Trent True lives in Kentucky and has been a tour guide, bookseller, teacher, and dispatcher. When he's not writing poetry or short stories, or making retro style digital illustrations, he's likely enjoying vintage sci fi films, pulp style radio programs, or dreaming of being a Roaring Twenties slam poet.

Maggi Vaughn is the author of twenty books. She has appeared in many anthologies and has received numerous awards. She is the Poet Laureate of Tennessee and resides in Bell Buckle, Tennessee.

Chuck Wagner has been an AP Literature and Creative Writing teacher at Brebeuf Jesuit for the last 24 years. He holds a Master of Arts in English from the University of Kansas and a Master of Fine Art in Creative Writing from Indiana University. He currently resides in Westfield, Indiana with his wife Shari and is the proud parent of two daughters, Vienna and Iona.

Shari Wagner, a former Indiana Poet Laureate, is the author of three books of poems: *The Farm Wife's Almanac* (forthcoming in May 2019), *The Harmonist at Nightfall,* and *Evening Chore.* She has an MFA from Indiana University and teaches for the Indiana Writers Center and IUPUI's Religion, Spirituality, and the Arts Initiative.

April Waldron lives in West Virginia and loves writng poetry and short stories. Her inspiration comes from her sons and grandson.

Ron Wallace is an Oklahoma native of Scots-Irish, Choctaw, Cherokee and Osage descent. He is currently an adjunct instructor of English at Southeastern Oklahoma State University, in Durant, Oklahoma, and is the author of nine books of poetry; five of which have been finalists in the Oklahoma Book Awards. *Renegade and Other Poems* was the 2018 winner of the Oklahoma Book Award, and his latest work, *The Last Blue Sky* is a current finalist in the 2019 Oklahoma Book Awards.

Jane Wheeler lives with her husband, horses, dogs, and cats on a hobby farm in Lowell, Michigan. She can throw a rope, if she doesn't have to catch anything, and enjoys poetry, cowboys, and booze equally.

Alessio Zanelli is an Italian poet who writes in English and whose work has appeared in over 150 journals from 13 countries. His fifth original collection, titled *The Secret Of Archery,* will be published in 2019 by Greenwich Exchange (London). For more information please visit www.alessiozanelli.it.

CPSIA information can be obtained
at www.ICGtesting.com
Printed in the USA
LVHW092150110419
613916LV00001B/362/P